KARL RAHNER

OUTSTANDING CHRISTIAN THINKERS

Series Editor: Brian Davies OP

The series offers a range of authoritative studies on people who have made an outstanding contribution to Christian thought and understanding. The series will range across the full spectrum of Christian thought to include Catholic and Protestant thinkers, to cover East and West, historical and contemporary figures. By and large, each volume will focus on a single 'thinker', but occasionally the subject may be a movement or a school of thought.

Brian Davies OP, the Series Editor, is Regent of Studies at Blackfriars, Oxford, where he also teaches philosophy. He is a member of the Theology Faculty at the University of Oxford and tutor at St Benet's Hall, Oxford. He has lectured regularly at the University of Bristol, Fordham University, New York, and the Beda College, Rome. He is Reviews Editor of *New Blackfriars*. His previous publications include: *An Introduction to the Philosophy of Religion* (OUP, 1982); *Thinking about God* (Geoffrey Chapman, 1985); *The Thought of Thomas Aquinas* (OUP, 1992); and he was editor of *Language, Meaning and God* (Geoffrey Chapman, 1987).

Already published:

The Apostolic Fathers
Simon Tugwell OP

Bultmann
David Fergusson

Denys the Areopagite
Andrew Louth

Reinhold Niebuhr
Kenneth Durkin

The Venerable Bede
Benedicta Ward SLG

Karl Rahner
William V. Dych SJ

Anselm
G. R. Evans

Hans Urs von Balthasar
John O'Donnell SJ

Teresa of Avila
Rowan Williams

Lonergan
Frederick E. Crowe SJ

Handel
Hamish Swanston

Yves Congar
Aidan Nichols OP

Planned titles in the series include:

Jonathan Edwards
John E. Smith

KARL RAHNER

William V. Dych SJ

A Michael Glazier Book
THE LITURGICAL PRESS
Collegeville, Minnesota

A Michael Glazier Book
published by The Liturgical Press
St John's Abbey, Collegeville, MN 56321, USA

Published in Great Britain by Geoffrey Chapman, an imprint of
Cassell Publishers Limited

First published 1992

Library of Congress Cataloging-in-Publication Data
A catalog record for this book is available from the Library of Congress

ISBN 0-8146-5053-8

Typeset by Colset Private Limited, Singapore
Printed and bound in Great Britain by
Biddles Ltd, Guildford and King's Lynn

Contents

Editorial foreword

St Anselm of Canterbury once described himself as someone with faith seeking understanding. In words addressed to God he says 'I long to understand in some degree thy truth, which my heart believes and loves. For I do not seek to understand that I may believe, but I believe in order to understand.'

And this is what Christians have always inevitably said, either explicitly or implicitly. Christianity rests on faith, but it also has content. It teaches and proclaims a distinctive and challenging view of reality. It naturally encourages reflection. It is something to think about; something about which one might even have second thoughts.

But what have the greatest Christian thinkers said? And is it worth saying? Does it engage with modern problems? Does it provide us with a vision to live by? Does it make sense? Can it be preached? Is it believable?

This series originates with questions like these in mind. Written by experts, it aims to provide clear, authoritative and critical accounts of outstanding Christian writers from New Testament times to the present. It will range across the full spectrum of Christian thought to include Catholic and Protestant thinkers, thinkers from East and West, thinkers ancient, mediaeval and modern.

The series draws on the best scholarship currently available, so it will interest all with a professional concern for the history of Christian ideas. But contributors will also be writing for general readers who have little or no previous knowledge of the subjects to be dealt with. Volumes to appear should therefore prove helpful at a popular as well as an academic level. For the most part they will be devoted to a single thinker, but occasionally the subject will be a movement or school of thought.

The subject of the present book, Karl Rahner (1904–84), is fairly described as the most important and influential Roman Catholic thinker of modern times. He exercised a profound influence at the Second Vatican Council. His theological writings run to an enormous number of volumes, many of which stand as classics in their field.

Nor was his work confined only to theology (considered as a technical or academic matter). He claimed not to have a philosophy, but he had a profound grasp of philosophical authors, whose insights he tried to apply to reflection on a wide range of topics of significance to all Christians. He was also concerned to show how theology bears on everyday life and ordinary Christian practice, as we can see from the large amount of time he devoted to works of 'popular' theology, and as we can also see from the impact upon him of the *Exercises* of St Ignatius Loyola.

In the pages which follow, William Dych, a student and friend of Rahner, lucidly displays all these aspects of Rahner's impressive legacy. The huge range and extent of Rahner's writings make it difficult for those approaching him for the first time to get an overview of his interests and ideas. Professor Dych's book, however, will set them solidly on their way. It is a concise, accurate and comprehensive account of Rahner's thinking from his student days to the time of his death. It consistently relates that thinking to the teachings of Vatican II, so readers will also readily see how Rahner should be located in the history of Roman Catholic teaching.

Brian Davies OP

Abbreviations

AG   *Ad Gentes.* Vatican II's Decree on the Church's Missionary
      Activity: *The Documents of Vatican II*, ed. Walter M.
      Abbott SJ (London: Geoffrey Chapman/New York: Herder
      & Herder, 1966). All references to Vatican II documents are
      from this edition.

DS   *Enchiridion Symbolorum Definitionum et Declarationum
      de Rebus Fidei et Morum*, ed. H. Denzinger, rev. A. Schön-
      metzer (Freiburg: Herder, 35th edn, 1973).

DV   *Dei Verbum.* Vatican II's Dogmatic Constitution on Divine
      Revelation.

FC   Karl Rahner, *Foundations of Christian Faith* (London:
      Darton, Longman & Todd/New York: Seabury, 1978).

GS   *Gaudium et Spes.* Vatican II's Pastoral Constitution on the
      Church in the Modern World.

HW   Karl Rahner, *Hearers of the Word* (London: Sheed & Ward/
      New York: Herder & Herder, 1969).

LG   *Lumen Gentium.* Vatican II's Dogmatic Constitution on the
      Church.

SM   Karl Rahner with Cornelius Ernst and Kevin Smyth (eds),
      Sacramentum Mundi: An Encyclopaedia of Theology, 6 vols
      (London: Burns & Oates/New York: Sheed & Ward, 1968–
      70).

SW   Karl Rahner, *Spirit in the World* (London: Sheed & Ward/
      New York: Herder & Herder, 1968).

TI   Karl Rahner, *Theological Investigations*, 22 vols (London:
      Darton, Longman & Todd/New York: Seabury/Crossroad,
      1961–91).

Introduction

When Karl Rahner died on 30 March 1984, just a few weeks after his eightieth birthday, he left a legacy of theological writings that is remarkable for its sheer volume as well as for the scope and variety of its contents. The bibliography of his books, articles and interviews, his sermons, prayers and meditations numbers between three and four thousand titles, and there is hardly a topic in Catholic theology to which he did not give his attention.[1] The breadth and depth of his vision have led some to call him the greatest Catholic thinker of this century, and to compare his achievement to that of Thomas Aquinas in his age.

To those who knew him personally the man was as remarkable as the theologian, and their esteem for him is matched by the affection with which they remember him. Perhaps what was so striking was that, though he spent his entire adult life in the university, theology for him was never an academic career. It was a way of life, a life of faith that was seeking understanding and seeking the words to convey that faith to others. Amidst the sceptics and agnostics of a secular age he was proud of his Christian heritage and always stood ready to give an account of it (see 1 Peter 3:15).

It is not surprising, then, that books and articles about him and his theology have abounded both before and since his death. Why, then, another book on Karl Rahner? Perhaps the best way for someone who was privileged to have Rahner as a teacher for five years to answer that question is to listen to some of his remarks about his own teachers and how he understood the process of 'learning' from them.

1

Since Karl Rahner was one of the most famous students of one of the most famous philosophers of our age, Martin Heidegger, he was often asked what he had learned from him and how Heidegger had influenced his own thought. 'I learned something about thinking itself, about how to think' is one of the variations of his usual reply, or 'He taught us how to read texts in a new way, to ask what is behind the text, to see connections . . . that would not immediately strike the ordinary person' or, finally, he taught us 'the courage to question anew so much in the tradition considered self-evident'. While not a Heideggerian, he expresses his thanks for Heidegger's help 'in the struggle to incorporate modern philosophy into today's Christian theology'.[2]

Likewise, when Rahner spoke of being a student of Thomas Aquinas and a Thomist, which he always claimed to be, he said that it was his own questions arising out of the present that prompted him to read the past. He wanted to interpret Aquinas not just as an historian would whose interest was the past, but as a philosopher concerned with the present, and always keeping an eye on the reality Thomas was talking about. Confronting the insights of Thomas with modern philosophy and its questions yields yet deeper insight into both. By this process of cross-fertilization classical philosophy of the Western tradition beginning with the Greeks, the *philosophia perennis*, remains a living truth addressing the present and does not become a dead letter from the past.[3]

In both teachers, then, Aquinas and Heidegger, it was not just the letter but also the spirit that intrigued him. A teacher does not supply answers, but teaches one how to question and how to search. By embodying their spirit and not just repeating the letter, the traditions they represent could be kept alive and fruitful. For this reason Rahner did not try to fashion a closed and finished theological system, but saw his theology as a moment in this larger and longer process. Even Church teaching must be seen not as an end but as a beginning, as he put it in a famous article on the Council of Chalcedon.[4] For theology, like the faith it reflects on, is a living process and, as Newman once said, 'to live is to change'.

What is true of all human knowledge is especially true of theology, for theology tries to speak of God, and God lies beyond the power of human speech. By its nature theology's agenda is always unfinished and its word incomplete. All theology ends in silence, as Rahner put it in the title of his little book, *Encounters with Silence*.[5] While paying close attention to the letter, then, to Rahner the theologian reflecting on his and his Church's faith, this book will also try to stay in touch with the spirit that animated it and with the man whose living faith sought expression in and for our time.

Notes

1   A bibliography of Rahner's works in English as well as secondary sources and a list of German bibliographies can be found in a special issue of *The Heythrop Journal* in honour of his eightieth birthday: 25, no. 3 (July 1984), pp. 319–60. It was compiled by C. J. Pedley SJ. A brief supplement, with a few corrections and additions, appears in 26 (1985), p. 310.

2   See Rahner's recollections in *I Remember: An Autobiographical Interview with Meinold Krauss* (New York: Crossroad/London: SCM, 1985), pp. 45, 47.

3   See Rahner's remarks on his method of interpreting Aquinas in the Introduction to SW, pp. xlix–lv. See also 'On recognizing the importance of Thomas Aquinas', TI 13, pp. 3–12.

4   See 'Current problems in Christology', TI 1, pp. 149–200.

5   *Encounters with Silence* (Westminster, MD: Newman, 1960/London: Burns & Oates, 1975).

1

The man and his work

Karl Rahner was born in Germany in the town of Freiburg in Breisgau on 5 March 1904.[1] He was one of seven children in what he described as 'a normal, middle-class Christian family'.[2] His father was a professor at the teachers' college in Freiburg. There was always something to eat, he recalled, but to support seven children his father had to tutor on the side and his mother baby-sat to bring in some extra money. He once told me that his mother's lifelong dream was to own her own home, but though she lived to be 101, her dream was never realized.

He attended primary and secondary school in Freiburg, where he described himself as an average pupil who found classes somewhat boring. On 20 April 1922, at the age of eighteen, and three weeks after finishing school, he entered the novitiate of the Society of Jesus which at that time was in Feldkirch, Austria. He was following in the footsteps of his older brother, Hugo, who had become a Jesuit three years earlier. As a novice he wrote his first article for the journal *Leuchtturm* ('Lighthouse') on a topic to which he was often to return, 'Why we need to pray' (1924). In later years he and his brother Hugo used to joke that one should publish much and publish early so that one had something to smile about in old age.

After finishing the two-year novitiate and taking his vows as a Jesuit, he began the normal course of studies for Jesuits at the time. He studied philosophy for three years, the first in Feldkirch and the second and third at the Jesuit philosophy school in Pullach, near Munich. Here he was introduced both to the scho-

4

lastic philosophy of the Catholic tradition and to modern German philosophy. His notebooks indicate a careful study of Kant and two contemporary Thomists, the Belgian Jesuit Joseph Maréchal (1878–1944) and the French Jesuit Pierre Rousselot (1878–1915), who were to have a profound influence on Rahner's own interpretation of Thomas Aquinas. He attributes to Maréchal his first real philosophical insight.[3]

It was the Jesuit custom to include a period of practical work between the study of philosophy and theology. Rahner was assigned to teach Latin to the novices at Feldkirch for two years. His complete command of Latin was to stand him in good stead in later years. Not only did it give him access to the Western tradition in philosophy and theology, but his fluent Latin was also his means of communication to non-German speakers at the Second Vatican Council and on many other occasions. I remember once on a visit to Hungary in 1969 a bishop asking Rahner quite unexpectedly after lunch to give a talk to his seminarians. Somewhat reluctantly he agreed, and to the seminarians assembled in their threadbare cassocks and tattered shoes he gave an impromptu and very moving talk in unfaltering Latin on the meaning of poverty, suffering and the cross.

With his first teaching behind him Rahner began his theological studies in 1929 at the Jesuit school of theology in Valkenburg, Holland. Though a new spirit in theology was already stirring in Germany in writers like Romano Guardini, Karl Adam and Erich Przywara, it did not penetrate seminary walls. There Rome's harsh and relentless battle against modernism, begun by Pius X at the beginning of the century, was still being waged vigorously between the two world wars. Courses in theology followed the prescribed method and prescribed terminology of a strict neo-Scholasticism which dictated not only the correct answers but also the correct questions. It was against this kind of theology that Rahner protested in later years with his frequent and sharp criticism of 'school theology'.

However, other parts of his theological studies were valuable and fruitful. He became thoroughly conversant with large areas of patristic theology by reading the Church Fathers on such topics as grace, sacraments, spirituality and mysticism.[4] His studies of the spiritual senses in Origen and Bonaventure led to his first major published articles in 1932 and 1933. Of special importance during this period were the studies he made in collaboration with his brother Hugo of the *Spiritual Exercises* of St Ignatius Loyola, the founder of the Jesuit Order. His early interest in the Ignatian notions of prayer, mysticism and existential decision-making became a lifelong preoccupation of such significance that he was able to say:

> But I think that the spirituality of Ignatius himself, which one learned through the practice of prayer and religious formation, was more significant for me than all learned philosophy and theology inside and outside the Order.[5]

On 26 July 1932, in the Jesuit church of St Michael in Munich, Karl Rahner, along with sixteen of his Jesuit brothers, was ordained priest by Cardinal Michael Faulhaber. He still had one year of his theological studies to complete, and after that he made his tertianship at St Andrea in Austria. Tertianship is the final year of Jesuit preparation, devoted to prayer and gaining pastoral experience, before embarking on one's active ministry. For Rahner it had been decided by his superiors in the Order that he was to teach the history of philosophy at Pullach. To prepare for this he returned to his home town of Freiburg in 1934 to do a doctorate in philosophy at the university. It was to be a time of opportunity and disappointment.

The opportunity presented itself in the presence of Martin Heidegger on the philosophy faculty, making Freiburg one of the most stimulating centres of philosophical studies in Germany at the time. However, during his term as rector of the university which had just ended, Heidegger had declared himself an enthusiastic supporter of Nazism. Although it is said that his ardour for the Nazis cooled thereafter, his politics made him a questionable choice as doctoral mentor for a Catholic and a priest. Rahner chose instead as his mentor Martin Honecker, who occupied the chair of Catholic philosophy. Nevertheless, he was able to attend Heidegger's seminars and found in his readings and interpretations of the pre-Socratics, Plato, Aristotle and Kant a genuine intellectual challenge and a philosophical experience for which he was always grateful.[6]

The choice of Honecker as doctoral mentor, however, ended ultimately in disappointment. Rahner chose as the topic for his dissertation a study of Thomas Aquinas's metaphysics of finite knowledge. Influenced by the interpretation of Thomas he had found in Maréchal and Rousselot, he wanted to do what he called a philosophical interpretation of the text.[7] By this he meant, for example, interpreting the Thomistic notion of the *excessus* or plus factor in human knowledge of the finite in the light of subsequent transcendental philosophy and its insights into the nature of human knowledge, allowing the two traditions to be mutually enriching. Thomas Aquinas, of course, did not know transcendental philosophy and did not have its insights in mind when he used the term *excessus*. But reading it in that light did throw new light on the text.

Honecker, however, did not read the text in that light, and the lights of one's dissertation director are all-important. His own interpretation was the more traditional scholastic one and he rejected the dissertation.[8] So ended Rahner's doctoral candidacy. By this time, however, he had left Freiburg and had begun doctoral studies in theology in Innsbruck. His superiors had reassigned him to teach theology in Innsbruck because of the retirement of some of the Jesuit professors there. Once while taking a walk with Rahner in Munich I asked him how disappointed he was when he received Honecker's rejection letter. 'I was not disappointed at all', he insisted. Had the dissertation been accepted he would have had to interrupt his theology studies, return to Freiburg and spend months preparing for and taking his comprehensive examinations to finish the doctorate. 'I was relieved to be delivered from that work', he said with a smile.

His doctoral studies in theology went more smoothly and conventionally. He returned to a topic that had interested him during his seminary theology, the typological interpretation of John 19:34 found in some of the Church Fathers. He quickly finished his dissertation, entitled 'The origin of the Church as Second Eve from the side of Christ the Second Adam. An investigation of the typological meaning of John 19:34', and received his doctorate towards the end of 1936. That along with his earlier published articles qualified him for an appointment to the theology faculty in Innsbruck, which he received on 1 July 1937. Not long after, the rejected Freiburg dissertation was published under the title *Geist in Welt*,[9] and translated into several languages including the English *Spirit in the World*. Not everyone shared Honecker's negative view of Rahner's interpretation of Thomas Aquinas.

Between his appointment to the theology faculty and the actual beginning of the winter term in October, Rahner delivered a series of fifteen lectures in Salzburg during the summer of 1937 which were to be extremely important in the development of his theology.

They were concerned with the philosophy of religion, and he applied the philosophy of knowledge developed in his Freiburg dissertation to the question of knowing God through an historical revelation. They were subsequently published under the title *Hörer des Wortes*,[10] translated into English as *Hearers of the Word*. These two books were the seminal and foundational works from out of which Rahner was to develop his philosophical theology.

The beginning of the winter term in 1937 was for Rahner the beginning of a career as professor of theology which was to last for 34 years. In a three-year cycle he covered the doctrines of creation and original sin, grace, justification, faith, hope and charity, and the sacraments of penance, anointing of the sick and orders. Innsbruck at the time was the centre of the development of what was called 'kerygmatic theology'. Karl's brother Hugo and the liturgist Josef Jungmann were deeply involved, and their intention was to provide for the students, along with their training in scholastic theology, a theology that could be preached as the former could not. The movement died an early death, aborted by Rome's unhappiness with what it saw as a threat to scholastic theology as the staple of seminary training.

Karl Rahner was also unhappy with kerygmatic theology, but for a different reason. He agreed entirely with the problem, that scholastic theology did not prepare students for pastoral work. But he did not think that the solution was to give the students a second and parallel theology. Something had to be done about scholastic theology. However academic and scientific a theology is, if it stays in touch with the faith upon which it is reflecting and close to life and reality, it will be able to be preached. As he put it, 'But in fact, the strictest theology, that most passionately devoted to reality alone and ever on the alert for new questions, the most scientific theology, is itself in the long run the most kerygmatic'.[11] This was the principle that was to guide Karl Rahner during his many years of teaching. Academic theology was not an end in itself, and the academy did not exist for its own sake, but to serve the Church's life of faith and its mission to preach God's word in the contemporary world.

Only a year after Rahner joined the theology faculty in Innsbruck its work was abruptly halted by political events in Austria. The Nazis had marched in and annexed Austria to Germany in March 1938, and a few months later they abolished the faculty of theology in Innsbruck. The Jesuits withdrew into their own college and continued their teaching there. This lasted only a year, until the college too was closed and the Jesuits banished from Innsbruck in October 1939. Some, including Hugo Rahner, went to Switzerland to try to keep the faculty intact. Karl Rahner was invited to Vienna, where he spent most of the war years as a member of the diocesan Pastoral Institute.

In Vienna he had a variety of teaching and lecturing opportunities, but one incident in particular should be mentioned. In January 1943, the then Archbishop of Freiburg wrote a 21-page letter to all the bishops of Germany and Austria warning them of dangerous innovations in Catholic doctrine and liturgy which he spelled out in 17 points.[12] The Archbishop of Vienna, Cardinal Innitzer, did not share his sentiments and entrusted his Pastoral Office with the drafting of a 53-page response which was written by Karl Rahner. Whatever the reaction of the German and Austrian bishops, all of whom received a copy, Rahner's response shows his acute sense of the need for the kind of reform in Church teaching and liturgy which was in fact undertaken 20 years later by the Second Vatican Council.

Rahner spent the last year of the war in the small Bavarian village of Mariakirchen as parish priest. This reveals a pastoral side of his work which continued through his life in frequent preaching and retreat-giving. The poignancy and depth of his preaching are well illustrated in a series of Lenten sermons he gave in the Jesuit church in Munich in 1946 on the need and blessing of prayer which were later published under the title *Not und Segen des Gebetes*.[13] His pastoral concern for people was evident in many ways, one of which I will mention. More than once I accompanied him, as did others, on a journey first to the supermarket where he would buy a large supply of groceries, and then on to some poor family which he had met perhaps years earlier but whose need he had not forgotten.

With the war over, Rahner returned to the reconstituted theology faculty in Innsbruck in 1948 and began an incredibly prolific period of writing and publishing. Articles which usually began as lectures abounded in many journals, and it was suggested to Rahner that they would reach a wider audience if he collected and published them in a single volume or two. In one of the ironies of his life, although in fact these volumes were eventually to reach sixteen in the German original and to be translated into other languages all over the world, including 22 volumes so far in English, he was not able to find a Catholic publisher in Germany interested in the project. Finally the Swiss publisher Benziger agreed and the first three volumes of *Schriften zur Theologie* appeared in 1954, 1955 and 1956.[14] The prolific career of Rahner the publicist was under way.

There was another side to Rahner's publishing that by itself would have been career enough for any man, his work as an editor. Here I will simply mention the major projects in which he was actively involved. In the 1950s he was the editor of the 28th to 31st editions of Denzinger's *Enchiridion Symbolorum*, the compendium of texts of the Church's official teaching. He was co-editor with Josef Höfer of a new edition of Herder's ten-volume *Lexikon für Theologie und Kirche* which appeared between 1957 and 1965. He edited with Adolf Darlap between 1967 and 1969 the six-volume *Sacramentum Mundi*, which also appeared in English, French, Spanish, Italian and Dutch, each entrusted to its own editor. During his summer vacation in 1961 Rahner produced along with Herbert Vorgrimler his *Concise Theological Dictionary*, which proved to be immensely popular.[15] He was also a co-editor of the *Handbook of Pastoral Theology* (five part-volumes, 1964–69) and an accompanying lexicon (1972), and of the 30-volume encyclopedia *Christian Faith in Modern Society* (1980–83). Rahner helped to plan the new compendium of dogmatic theology, *Mysterium Salutis*, which appeared in five volumes between 1965 and 1976. In addition to editing, he also contributed many articles to these various volumes.

There was one project very dear to Rahner's heart that deserves separate mention. Even before the war he was convinced of the need to dispel the notion that Catholic theology was a monolith in which everything of importance was settled, and therefore he saw the need for a forum in which disputed questions could be discussed and progress in theology could be made. This idea became reality when in 1958 the first volume appeared in a new series entitled *Quaestiones Disputatae*, edited by Karl Rahner and the New Testament scholar Heinrich Schlier.[16] He published eight of his own books in this series and co-authored another eight. Shortly before his death the series reached its 101st volume. With this same concern in mind he helped to found the international theological journal *Concilium* and edited the first number with Edward Schillebeeckx in 1965. He hoped that its simultaneous publication in six languages would give the Church a worldwide forum for theological discussion.

While busily engaged in these more scholarly pursuits, Rahner's more pastoral activities and concerns did not diminish. A glance at his bibliography shows that during these years he was also occupied with pastoral theology, and in 1959 he published 24 articles on a variety of pastoral topics under the title *Sendung und Gnade*.[17] There also appeared collections of his sermons, prayers and the meditations he gave while conducting the *Spiritual Exercises* of St Ignatius.[18] During these Innsbruck years Rahner was also an active member of several learned societies in Germany concerned with questions of Christian ecumenism and the relation of faith and science. He was to leave Innsbruck for Munich in 1963, but several events should be mentioned before considering that move.

Not everyone saw the need for theological renewal as Rahner did, nor were they happy with the direction his theology was taking and the widening sphere of his influence. The first difficulty he encountered was in 1951 when he was refused permission to publish a lengthy manuscript entitled 'Problems of contemporary Mariology'. He was prompted to write it by the promulgation in 1950 by Pius XII of the dogma of the Assumption of Mary, a doctrine not mentioned in Scripture nor mentioned in extant Church writings until the fifth century. Rahner did not question the dogma nor the legitimacy of its promulgation. He did, however, think that it raised important questions about the nature of Tradition and the development of doctrine, particularly from an ecumenical point of view. It seems that the censor, a fellow-Jesuit at the Gregorian University in Rome, E. Dhanis, had serious reservations and the manuscript was never published.

Rahner had also written a long article in 1949 which he called 'The many Masses and the one sacrifice'.[19] In it he raised a variety of questions about the relationship between the Masses celebrated by the Church and the sacrifice of the cross they make present, about the 'fruits of the Mass' and the value of multiplying the number of Masses, and about the possibility of concelebration for priests, something now taken for granted. In a public statement in 1954 Pius XII, without mentioning Rahner by name, took issue with what he thought Rahner had said, and he was then forbidden by the Holy Office to discuss the issue of concelebration in the future.[20] Years later I remember leaving the Vatican with Rahner who had just emerged from a private audience with Paul VI. He had reminded the Pope of the prohibition, and then said jokingly 'Today you concelebrate more often than I do'. The Pope smiled and said 'Est tempus flendi, est tempus ridendi' ('There is a time to weep and a time to laugh'). Rahner's article was just a bit ahead of its time.

Another article in 1960 caused serious problems in Rome.[21] In it Rahner raised questions about the Catholic doctrine of the perpetual virginity of Mary during and after the birth of Jesus. He distinguished between what is the real content and substance of a doctrine, and what can be considered part of the historically conditioned form in which it is expressed. Despite rumors of impending steps to be taken against Rahner, for the time being, at least, nothing happened.

However, two years later, without warning and with no specific reason given, Rahner received word from his Jesuit superiors that henceforth everything he wrote had to be submitted to Rome for prior censorship. This was in 1962, around the same time when several Jesuits at the Pontifical Biblical Institute in Rome were being subjected to intense doctrinal scrutiny. On 23 June Rahner went to Rome to see the Jesuit General, who was sympathetic, but explained that he was simply handing on the order from the Holy Office. Rahner considered the measure against him unjust, and said that if it remained in force he would do no further writing.[22]

Fortunately, many quarters rallied to his support. In late June the three German-speaking Cardinals, Döpfner in Munich, Frings in Cologne and König in Vienna, sent a joint letter to the Pope asking that the prior censorship be lifted, and König spoke with the Pope personally. Perhaps of equal importance was a petition drawn up by the Paulusgesellschaft, a learned society of German professors in the sciences and humanities which was shocked at the implications of Rome's action. About 250 signatures were gathered and the petition was sent to Rome through diplomatic channels. Nothing happened immediately, but on 28 May 1963, Rahner was informed by the Jesuit General that the special censorship had been dropped and that he need only follow the same procedures as everyone else in the Order. Rahner reported an earlier conversation with Cardinal Ottaviani, then head of the Holy Office, in which he asked him about the censorship. Ottaviani explained that it was merely to protect him from friends who misunderstood him, and should be seen as a privilege. Rahner was happy to forgo such privileges.

During this time momentous events were happening in Rome which were to change the whole climate for Rahner and other theologians of reform. In 1959 Pope John XXIII had announced his plan to convene an ecumenical council at the Vatican, and in 1960 preparatory commissions were established to plan the agenda and draw up the preliminary documents. Rahner played only a very minor role in this preparatory work. One of the requests received by the commission was for the restoration of the permanent diaconate, and since Rahner had written on the matter he was appointed an adviser to the relevant commission on this limited question. Of much more importance was his selection by Cardinal König in Vienna to be his private adviser on all the Council documents, a role he also played for Cardinal Döpfner.

On 11 October 1962, the Council was solemnly opened and later that month Rahner was appointed one of the official *periti*, or theological experts of the Council. This gave him access to the Council sessions in St Peter's, but he did his real work and had his real influence at the Council outside the official sessions. He addressed the German-speaking bishops and other regional bishops' groups as well, and took part in the discussions of the German and French theologians. For example, on the thorny and controversial question of Scripture and Tradition as sources of revelation, he and Joseph Ratzinger prepared an alternate text to the one submitted by the preparatory commission and it was accepted by the German bishops' conference. The call by John XXIII on 21 November 1962 for a new text on revelation was a real watershed for the Council, for it opened the way for a thorough revision of all the texts that had been prepared in Rome beforehand.

There is no doubt that by the time the Council ended in December 1965 Rahner had exercised enormous influence on the final shape of many of the conciliar documents. Traces of his theology can be found in the Council's teaching on the Church, on papal primacy and the episcopate, on revelation and the relationship between Scripture and Tradition, on the inspiration of the Bible, on the sacraments and the diaconate, on the relationship of the Church to the modern world, on the possibility of salvation outside the Church even for non-believers, and in many other areas. It is ironic that the ideas of a theologian who only recently had been highly suspect and subject to special censorship had now become part of the Church's official teaching. Not only did the Second Vatican Council end Rahner's official difficulties with Rome, but it also gave him international stature as one of the Church's leading theologians.

During the time of the Council in Rome there was also a significant change for Rahner at home. The University of Munich was seeking a successor to Romano Guardini in the chair of Christianity and the Philosophy of Religion, and in February 1963 asked Rahner if he would be interested. He had earlier been invited by the University of Münster to teach dogmatic theology there, but the Jesuit General preferred that he remain in Innsbruck. This time

Rahner was eager to accept the invitation, among other reasons because he felt that the move to a German university would provide greater protection against such things as the Roman censorship measure. German universities were also more generous in providing their professors with the help of assistants than was the case in Jesuit seminaries.

On his sixtieth birthday, 5 March 1964, Rahner was appointed to the chair in Munich with the consent of his Jesuit superiors. One of the courses he gave there over two semesters was subsequently published under the title *Grundkurs des Glaubens: Einführung in den Begriff des Christentums*.[23] Although the book is not a summary of Rahner's theology, it comes closer than any of his other publications to giving a unified and systematic view of his thought. Rahner was to remain in Munich only three years, mainly because he was, and wished to remain, a theologian and many of his students came to Munich to study theology. But his chair was in the philosophy faculty, and the theology faculty refused to grant him equal rights to present candidates for degrees in theology.

The University of Münster was still very interested in having Rahner come there and this time, given the anomalous situation in Munich, he accepted their invitation. On 1 April 1967, he was appointed to what was to be his final teaching position as professor of dogmatic theology in Münster. Rahner was happy to be back teaching theology, but by 1971, in his sixty-eighth year and with his physical strength declining, he had had enough teaching and decided to retire from the university and return to the Jesuit writers' house in Munich.

Retirement, however, did not change a great deal in Rahner's life. He was as busy as ever writing and lecturing both in Germany and abroad, and remained so until the time of his death thirteen years later. In 1981 he was invited back to Innsbruck by the Jesuits there, who offered him the rooms which were to become the Rahner Archive. In the autumn of that year he returned to Innsbruck and mentioned in a note to me shortly thereafter that he was happy to be back. It was in Innsbruck that he had spent his most productive years and had experienced the dramatic changes of the Second Vatican Council. By contrast, Rahner described the present as a 'wintry season', a season of disappointment at what he perceived to be the not fully realized promise of the Council.[24]

As Rahner's eightieth birthday approached in 1984 honours and celebrations were being planned in many places. On 11 and 12 February he was invited back to his home town by the Catholic

Academy of Freiburg for a two-day conference in the packed Auditorium Maximum of the university. He then went to Heythrop College, in the University of London, and after that to the Budapest Academy in Hungary. All of this was preliminary to the celebration on his actual birthday, 5 March, in Innsbruck, where Lukas Vischer of the World Council of Churches gave the festive address.

Only three days after the celebrations Rahner fell ill with what was thought at first to be sheer exhaustion. The doctor ordered complete rest, and he spent the next three weeks in a sanitorium near Innsbruck. After a few days of rest he tried to take a daily walk, but even this proved too much and he had to abandon the attempt. In spite of his weak condition, he managed during this time to write a letter to the bishops of Peru supporting Gustavo Gutiérrez and his liberation theology. When his condition grew steadily worse he was moved to the University Medical Clinic in Innsbruck on 29 March. He died there the following evening, 30 March 1984. Many who had gathered for the birthday celebration just weeks before now returned to Innsbruck to mourn at his funeral in the Jesuit church of the Trinity where he now lies buried.

Notes

1 For some of the biographical details mentioned below I am indebted to two books of Herbert Vorgrimler, *Understanding Karl Rahner: An Introduction to his Life and Thought* (New York: Crossroad/London: SCM, 1986), and *Karl Rahner: His Life, Thought and Works* (London: Burns & Oates, 1965/Glen Rock, NJ: Paulist, 1966).

2 *I Remember*, p. 24.

3 *Karl Rahner in Dialogue: Conversations and Interviews 1965–1982*, ed. Paul Imhof and Hubert Biallowons, tr. and ed. Harvey Egan (New York: Crossroad, 1986), p. 14.

4 For a detailed study of this period see K.H. Neufeld, 'Unter Brüdern: zur Frühgeschichte der Theologie K. Rahners aus der Zusammenarbeit mit H. Rahner' in *Wagnis Theologie*, ed. H. Vorgrimler (Freiburg: Herder, 1979), pp. 341–54.

5 *Karl Rahner in Dialogue*, p. 191.

6 *I Remember*, pp. 45, 47.

7 See the Introduction to SW, pp. xliv–lv.

8 *I Remember*, p. 43.

9 *Geist in Welt* (Innsbruck: Felizian Rauch, 1939; 296 pp.). Rahner entrusted the preparation of a 2nd edition to J.B. Metz, who expanded the text considerably. It was published in Munich by Kösel in 1957 (414 pp.). It is this edition that was translated into English.

10 *Hörer des Wortes* (Munich: Kösel, 1941; 229 pp.). J. B. Metz also prepared a 2nd and revised edition of this work which was published by Kösel in 1963 (221 pp.). It is this edition which was translated into English.

11 'The prospects for dogmatic theology', TI 1, p. 7.

12 A detailed summary of the Archbishop's letter and Rahner's response is given in Vorgrimler's *Karl Rahner: His Life, Thought and Works*, pp. 32–42, and a much shorter account in his *Understanding Karl Rahner*, pp. 68–9.

13 *Not und Segen des Gebetes* (Freiburg: Herder, 1977).

14 The English translations of *Schriften zur Theologie* (Einsiedeln: Benziger, 1954–84) began to appear in 1961 under the title *Theological Investigations* (cited in this book as TI).

15 English translation: Karl Rahner and Herbert Vorgrimler, *Concise Theological Dictionary* (London: Burns & Oates, 1963; 2nd edn, 1983).

16 The *Quaestiones Disputatae* series was translated into English under the same title by Burns & Oates in London and Herder & Herder in New York.

17 *Sendung und Gnade* (Innsbruck: Tyrolia, 1959; 561 pp.). The sub-title is *Contributions to Pastoral Theology*. The English translation appeared as *Mission and Grace*, vols 1–3 (London: Sheed & Ward, 1963–66)/*The Christian Commitment*; *Theology for Renewal: Bishops, Priests and Laity*; and *Christian in the Market Place* (New York: Sheed & Ward, 1963–66).

18 See, for example, *Biblical Homilies* (London: Burns & Oates/New York: Herder & Herder, 1966); *The Eternal Year* (London: Burns & Oates/Baltimore: Helicon, 1964); *Everyday Things* (London: Sheed & Ward, 1965); and *Spiritual Exercises* (New York: Herder & Herder, 1965/London: Sheed & Ward, 1967).

19 *Die vielen Messen und das eine Opfer* (Freiburg: Herder, 1951). Rahner refers to the controversy that the book aroused in the Preface to the English edition, *The Celebration of the Eucharist* (London: Burns & Oates/New York: Herder & Herder, 1968).

20 The Pope's comments appear in *Acta Apostolicae Sedis* 46 (1954), pp. 668–70.

21 'Virginitas in partu', *Schriften zur Theologie* 4 (1960), pp. 173–205; TI 4, pp. 134–62.

22 In an appendix to his *Understanding Karl Rahner*, Herbert Vorgrimler includes correspondence he had with Rahner at this time. For Rahner's reaction, see ibid., pp. 148ff.

23 *Grundkurs des Glaubens: Einführung in den Begriff des Christentums* (Freiburg: Herder, 1976); *Foundations of Christian Faith: Introduction to the Idea of Christianity* (New York: Seabury, London: Darton, Longman & Todd, 1978).

24 See Karl Rahner, *Faith in a Wintry Season: Conversations and Interviews with Karl Rahner in the Last Years of His Life*, ed. Paul Imhof and Hubert Biallowons, tr. and ed. Harvey Egan (New York: Crossroad, 1990), pp. 189–200.

2

Beyond gnosticism and agnosticism

On a visit to Fordham University in New York where he was awarded an honorary degree in 1980, Karl Rahner was asked during a colloquium with some members of the philosophy and theology faculties to say a few words about his philosophy. 'Ich habe keine Philosophie', 'I do not have a philosophy' was his simple response. He was making not just a modest disclaimer, but an important point about his method in doing theology. Looking at the chronology of his publications, where his first book was on the philosophy of knowledge and the second on the philosophy of religion,[1] one could have the opposite (and false) impression that Rahner first worked out a philosophical basis, and then built his theology upon it. In an important lecture which he gave at the University of Bamberg in 1977, but which first appeared in English the year of his death in 1984,[2] Rahner rejects such an understanding for both theological and philosophical reasons, as falsely portraying the relationship between faith and theology on the one hand, and knowledge in the sense of reason or philosophy on the other.

If theology is to remain true to its nature and speak of God in an authentically Christian way, he says, it must begin by questioning what knowledge has come to mean in our culture. Rahner describes this 'modern ideal of knowledge':

Knowledge achieves its true nature and reaches its goal only when it sees through and thus dominates what is known, when it breaks it down into what is for us unquestionable and obvious, when it seeks to work only with clear ideas . . . when it is interested only

18

in the functional connections of the details of the world of its experience...[3]

To deepen our understanding of knowledge as including more than 'the power of comprehending, of gaining mastery and subjugating', knowledge must be understood more fundamentally precisely as that wherein we stand before what is incomprehensible, as 'the capacity to be grasped' by what lies always beyond us, or in the terminology of Aquinas, 'as the capacity of *excessus*, of going out into the inaccessible'.[4]

In knowledge, says Rahner, our reach always exceeds our grasp, and however much we grasp, it is but a small island in the vast sea of what we do not know, and *know* that we do not know.[5] Indeed, the more we know, the more we realize how little we know. Pushing back the frontiers of knowledge does not lessen our sense of awe and wonder at the mystery of things, but deepens and enhances it. True knowledge, that is, knowledge which includes the larger and deeper truth about ourselves, knowledge which has also become wisdom, does not inflate and puff up, but humbles the knower. It is only a little learning that is a dangerous thing.

Rahner is not questioning either the reality or the value of the knowledge which by grasping and comprehending gains mastery and control over things. The accomplishments of modern science and technology stand as its undeniable tribute. Likewise, the development of modern methods of historical investigation and the tools of exegesis have greatly expanded our knowledge of the past, including our Christian past. He questions only its exclusive claim to be the only or the most fundamental kind of human knowledge, and points to this larger sense of the ultimate mystery of things as a qualitatively different kind of knowing and as an abiding ingredient permeating all our knowledge and all our everyday activities.[6]

Before looking at the theological reasons Rahner gives for insisting on this more comprehensive understanding of knowledge, it is important to notice two immediate consequences for faith and theology. If knowledge did indeed only mean to grasp and comprehend, it would appear that it is only at the end of this process of understanding through philosophical analysis or scientific investigation, at the point where reason with its logic and clarity runs out, that revelation would play its role and one would move into faith and theology. Likewise in the situation of the historian or the exegete, it would be at the end of the investigation by historical or exegetical methods, when historical or exegetical reason can go no further, that faith and theology begin.

The difficulty in both instances is that faith appears to be something which follows knowledge and fills in its gaps, whether it be the gaps of philosophical and scientific knowledge or the gaps of historical and exegetical knowledge. Faith and theology become a second-class kind of knowledge for those who are not hard-headed enough to stay with the evidence. This is the understanding of faith held by many contemporary agnostics who see their agnosticism as more intellectually honest. On their terms it probably is, which is why Rahner wants to question their terms and their understanding of knowledge. As he puts it when speaking of the relationship of faith to secular knowledge:

> We may say that today theology and faith must reflect upon their place of origin, which lies deeper and more fundamentally in human existence, prior to the plurality of ways of understanding the world and existence. Thus theology can and must be seen as the study of faith at a level prior to that of the secular sciences, speaking to man before he 'goes out' into the unintegrable pluralism which is his existence and his world ... This may provide the impetus to a new and more original self-interpretation of theology.[7]

That of which faith and theology speak is present at the beginning, not the end of the knowledge process, and they should be seen not as 'amplifying' secular knowledge and surpassing it, but as its 'slender root' and 'deeper source'.[8]

Lying at the other end of the spectrum to agnosticism is gnosticism. As the term 'gnosis' implies, the gnostic claims to know what is hidden to others and finds salvation through such knowledge. The knowledge, of course, is derived not through reason in any of its forms, but through secret revelations. While the gnostic thus seems to be the polar opposite to the agnostic, they both share the presupposition that Rahner is rejecting, that the theoretical contents of knowledge and the certain possession of those contents, whose possibility is affirmed by the gnostic and denied by the agnostic, are what is constitutive of knowledge. Knowledge, for both, is grasping something and being in sure possession of it. There is always the danger that genuine faith will be seen as an increment or 'amplification', as Rahner says above, to knowledge in the usual sense, and hence as a gnosis making up for the limitations of knowledge.

Rahner takes great pains to distinguish the Christian notion of revelation and the response of faith from such a gnostic under-

standing. When speaking of revelation in the context of the hiddenness of God he says:

> Divine revelation is not the unveiling of something previously
> hidden, which through this illumination leads to an awareness
> similar to that found in ordinary knowledge of the world. Rather
> it means that the 'deus absconditus' becomes radically present
> as the abiding mystery . . . Revelation does not mean that the
> mystery is overcome by gnosis bestowed by God, even in the direct
> vision of God; on the contrary, it is the history of the deepening
> perception of God *as* mystery.[9]

It is in this shared presumption about the nature of knowledge, in
the 'predominance of the desire for theoretical understanding',[10]
that any form of gnosticism and contemporary agnosticism meet:

> In such an ideal of knowledge the Greek desire of absolute gnosis
> and the modern understanding of knowledge as a process which
> leads to the mastery of an object come together, whether the
> mastery in question is conceived in terms of German idealism or
> of the natural sciences.[11]

In his understanding of the knowledge of God Rahner wants to
move beyond both gnosticism and agnosticism. Why do Christian
faith and theology make this move necessary?

Beginning in the Old and New Testaments, for example, in Paul's
description of God's saving action in Christ as impenetrable and
'inscrutable' (Rom 11:33), it has been the constant teaching of the
Christian tradition that God is incomprehensible and ineffable.[12]
This refers not only to God's nature or essence, but also to God's
freedom and action in the world: 'For my thoughts are not your
thoughts, neither are your ways my ways, says the Lord' (Isa 55:8).
According to this traditional teaching it is also true to say:

> The incomprehensibility of God persists also in the immediate
> face-to-face vision of God: that is, it is not merely something
> peculiar to the knowledge of God in the pilgrim's earthly life,
> but also determines our relationship to God in its eternal
> consummation.[13]

Moreover, the incomprehensibility of the God we encounter is
not merely one of God's attributes among others, a 'marginal

phenomenon', but 'the attribute of his attributes', the 'starting point which always and everywhere determines our understanding of God's nature and its peculiar and unique character'.[14]

But in spite of this long tradition, the truth that God is mystery is not always operative in theology, indeed, it tends to be forgotten at crucial points:

> This forgetting of God's incomprehensibility at the point where we recognize God as ultimate, sole and all-illuminating answer to man's radical question of meaning seems to me to be blatant. For us the person who does not know God is wandering in darkness; but the person who knows God walks in the light, and brings God into his calculations for living as the item that throws light on all the rest of his accounts.[15]

It is quite true to say that God gives meaning to life, indeed, is the meaning of life, but it becomes false when we spontaneously think of meaning in *our* sense: something *we* see and understand, something which is justified in *our* sight and makes sense *to us*. God then becomes a function within our calculations, an idol of our own creation to satisfy our needs, and this kind of gnosticism easily becomes agnosticism when God no longer 'works'. Where does theology find the authentic way of existing before God, revealing at once who God is and who we are?

The starting point for theology's talk, both about God and ourselves, is Jesus of Nazareth. In one of his definitions of theology Rahner puts it this way:

> Theology consists in a process of human reflection upon the revelation of God in Jesus Christ and, arising from this, upon the faith of the Church.[16]

First and foremost, then, theology is not reflection on doctrines in the sense of a body of knowledge or ideas to be mastered, but reflection on a person. Interpreting in this light Anselm's definition of theology as *fides quaerens intellectum*, faith seeking understanding, the understanding involved is not grasping an idea in what Rahner called the modern notion of knowledge, but is primarily the knowledge of a person. Christian faith and theology begin not with the process of investigating and grasping some*thing*, but by being grasped by some*one*. Rahner specifies this more precisely in a variety of ways in different contexts.

When speaking of Christology and the need to justify what the Church has said about Jesus in the lengthy development of its Christological doctrines, he says that 'the basic and decisive point of departure, of course, lies in an encounter with the historical Jesus of Nazareth'.[17] For this reason, he insists that doing Christology in the sense of reflection on the Church's doctrines requires as its basis and starting point what Rahner calls an 'existentiell Christology', by which he means a 'personal relationship to Jesus Christ'.[18] When speaking of faith in more general terms at the beginning of his study of the 'Foundations of Christian Faith', he says that such a study presumes 'the existence of our own personal Christian faith'.[19] Theology as reflection on faith means in the first instance reflection on lived faith or on the life of faith.

Encountering Jesus as a person before reflecting on the content of doctrines about him means beginning not with the Jesus or Christ of faith, but with the faith of Jesus himself as the New Testament gives witness to this. Heeding the summons of the letter to the Hebrews that we look to Jesus as 'the pioneer and perfecter of our faith' (12:2), Rahner finds in the faith of Jesus the foundation for the Jesus of faith. Reflecting on the implications of the 'hiddenness of God' for our understanding of Jesus, he says of the death of Jesus:

Jesus stands as a human being in faith before the inexorable mystery which becomes an object of love precisely in its incomprehensibility. This makes it intelligible that his death is not just one of a series of events in his human life, but is the climax of his existence. For as long as a person accepts death unconditionally in faith and hope, that person comes naked before the incomprehensibility of God, since all else has been destroyed.[20]

Earlier Christology was reluctant to ascribe faith to Jesus since this seemed incompatible with his divinity, and was inclined 'to ascribe as much positive and specific knowledge as possible to the mind of Jesus'. In Rahner's approach, on the other hand:

It would in fact be more important to stress the humanity of Jesus and emphasize that he surrendered himself unconditionally in his mind to the incomprehensibility of God and accepted with love, and without any attempt at repression, the ultimate 'beata ignorantia'. Seen in this light, the ignorance of Jesus, for which there is ample evidence in Scripture, does not point to a deficiency, but rather to a positive merit in his acceptance of this ignorance.[21]

Seeing Jesus as the 'pioneer and perfecter' of faith provides the paradigm for understanding the faith of his followers.

These texts mention two other scriptural terms besides faith which describe this relationship of Jesus to his Father, namely, hope and love, and Rahner looks at the relationship from each of these aspects. Hope, he says, 'is the name of an attitude in which we dare to commit ourselves to that which is radically beyond all human control'.[22] This 'letting go of the self' is the opposite to any attempt to control our destiny and have it at our own disposal. It is the recognition and acceptance that the future, here and hereafter, is in God's hands. 'In the word "hope" this one unifying attitude of "outwards from self" and into God as the absolutely uncontrollable finds expression.'[23] It is in this sense of hope that Paul says 'faith, hope, love abide, these three' (1 Cor 13:13), for hope describes a disposition that belongs not just to our time of pilgrimage on earth, to be replaced one day by possession, but an abiding element in our relationship to God.

As with faith, Rahner finds the foundation for and paradigm of this attitude and disposition in Jesus of Nazareth. The Jesus of our hope is based on the hope of Jesus himself. The presence of God's grace in the world, the foundation of hope, 'finds its unique historical manifestation in Christ precisely as *crucified*, and thereby as surrendering himself in the most radical sense to the disposing hand of God'.[24] Commenting on Luke's portrait of the death of Jesus (23:46), Rahner says:

> It is in this historical manifestation that the grace we are considering here definitively establishes itself in the world. But precisely this takes place in the death of Christ as the most radical act of hope ('Into *thy* hands I deliver up my life').[25]

The two attitudes which are opposed to hope, presumption and despair, 'are, at basis, the refusal of the subject to allow himself to be grasped by the uncontrollable and to be drawn out of himself by it'.[26] These two opposite attitudes are to hope what gnosticism and agnosticism are to faith.

The third aspect of Jesus' relationship to the Father is the one Paul calls the greatest: 'So faith, hope, love abide, these three; but the greatest of these is love' (1 Cor 13:13). Rahner stresses that

'Christianity is faith, hope and love', and these 'are not three realities related only extrinsically, each with its own origin and nature', but rather 'love is the one word for the fulfilment of the single reality that we signify by these three names'.[27] He sees the pre-eminence of love lying in the fact that in the face of God's incomprehensibility all of our knowledge must surpass and transcend itself into self-surrendering love in order to reach the deepest truth of knowledge:

> The act in which a person can face and accept the mystery of God (and therein the comprehensive meaning of his own existence), without being shattered by it and without fleeing from it into the banality of his clear and distinct ideas, the banality of looking for meaning based solely on such knowledge and what it can master and control, this act, I say, is the act of love in which a person surrenders and entrusts himself to this very mystery. In this love knowledge transcends itself to reach its own deepest nature, and truly becomes knowledge only by becoming love.[28]

If knowledge does not achieve its own perfection by being subsumed into love, 'it can only founder on the alien and inhospitable rock of God's incomprehensibility'.[29] But if the fundamental character of knowledge is not to 'see through' and master an object, but indeed to be subsumed into love, then we can regard knowledge in the former and usual sense 'as a derivation of the basic meaning of knowledge'.[30] At this deeper level of the 'perichoresis' or mutual interpenetration of knowledge and love, of the true and the good, Rahner finds a way beyond the traditional scholastic question of the primacy of intellect or will by seeing them in their original differentiated unity.[31]

An analogy from our everyday experience can clarify what is meant here:

> At the point where one person encounters another in really personal love is there not an acceptance of what is not comprehended, an acceptance of what we have not ourselves perceived and consequently not mastered in the other person, the person who is loved? Is not personal love a trusting surrender to the other person without guarantees, precisely in so far as the latter is and remains free and incalculable?[32]

Although another person can, indeed, become the object of knowledge in the sense of an object to be studied and understood, in interpersonal knowledge the other is known in his or her subjectivity and freedom, and this kind of knowledge includes trust and love. The fruit of such knowledge is not mastery of what is known, but union with what is known.

This analogy is also helpful as a reminder that our relationship to other persons not only throws light on our relationship to God, but also mediates that relationship. Commenting on the response of Jesus to the question about the greatest commandment in the law, that one must love God and one's neighbour as oneself (Matt 22:34–40; Mark 12:28–31; Luke 10:25–28), Rahner points out that the commandment must not be understood in an extrinsic or arbitrary sense, as though God could have chosen some other commandment to be the most important. Rather the commandment expresses what is by its very nature constitutive of Christian existence.[33] Moreover, the commandment does not speak of two separate loves, for love of another person 'is the mediation of the love of God and forms an ultimately inseparable unity with it'.[34] As he puts it in another text:

It can really be said seriously that love of God and love of neighbour are one, and it is in this way and only in this way that we understand who God and His Christ are. We love God in Christ when we allow our love of neighbour to realize its true nature and reach its true fulfillment.[35]

Rahner looks to Scripture for the ultimate basis of the unity of these two loves.

There is, first of all, the parable in Matthew's gospel (25:31–46) about the last day when the Son of Man will summon those on his right into his kingdom and send away those on his left. It is striking that 'the only norm that appears explicitly by which people will be judged is love of one's neighbour'.[36] Also in the synoptic tradition is 'the puzzling saying that what is done to the least of his brothers is done to Jesus, a saying that is not explained by assuming that Jesus is asserting an arbitrary, altruistic identification, an "as if" in a merely moral–juridical sense'.[37] Finally, Rahner points to the Johannine tradition:

Because God, who is love (1 Jn 4:16), has loved us, John draws the conclusion, not that we love God in return, but that we love one another (1 Jn 4:7, 11). For we do not see God, and God cannot truly be reached only in a gnostic and mystical interiority. John concludes: whoever does not love his brother whom he sees cannot love God whom he has not seen (1 Jn 4:20).[38]

From the synoptic and Johannine traditions Rahner concludes:

> It is true in a radical sense, that is, with an ontological necessity, not merely a 'moral' or psychological necessity, that whoever does not love his brother whom he 'sees' cannot love God whom he does not see, and one can only love God who is not seen by loving one's brother who is seen.[39]

Love for our neighbour, therefore, provides not just the analogy for understanding our relationship to God, but is also the concrete mediation of that relationship.

This kind of unity is also true of our hope in and for God. This hope is not separate from, but, like love, exists in unity with and is mediated by our present situation in the world. Commenting on the teaching of the Second Vatican Council's Dogmatic Constitution on the Church (no. 35), that hope in God's eschatological future must not be hidden in the innermost depths of the heart, but must be given concrete expression in the complexities and in the framework of secular life, Rahner says:

> Surely we would misunderstand this if we sought to interpret it merely as a moralising conclusion of a secondary kind, following from the nature of that hope which the 'sons of the promise' could, ultimately speaking, have lived by even without 'informing' the secular framework of the world with their hope in this way. Contrary to this view, the admonition contains a statement about an element which is essential to hope itself. The process by which this becomes an achieved reality involves a permanent transformation of the framework of secular life.[40]

Christian hope, as trusting in God's promise and not in our own power, involves his promise for here as well as for hereafter.

Christian hope, then, is not an interior attitude or an idea or theory about the future, but is embodied in the present and affects the present through 'interaction with the world of our environment and of our fellow human beings'.[41] Contrary to what people both inside and outside the Christian Church think about hope:

It is not the 'opium of the people' which soothes them in their present circumstances even though they are painful. Rather it is that which commands them, and at the same time empowers them, to have trust enough constantly to undertake anew an exodus out of the present into the future (even within the dimensions of this world).[42]

As with the unity of the love of God and neighbour, hope in and for God's future does not weaken, but strengthens one's bond with the present. For Jesus proclaimed that the kingdom of God in which he hoped was 'at hand' (Mark 1:15; Matt 4:17).

Looking at the life of Jesus of Nazareth, then, one can conclude with Rahner that Christianity in the first instance *is* faith, hope and love, or better, the active process of believing, hoping and loving. These three aspects of the single basic dynamism of Christian life do not constitute an answer to the mystery of God or to the mystery of life, but a response to this mystery. They are not in the first instance a theory, but a way of life. Each of them is an aspect of that single movement of 'letting go of the self' or self-transcendence which is not a movement out of the world, but through the world towards God.[43] In the language of Jesus as recorded in the New Testament, this process of self-transcendence is called the process of losing oneself or one's life in order to find it anew (Mark 8:35; Matt 10:39; Luke 17:33; John 12:25). The New Testament portrays Jesus as not only saying this but doing it in his life and death. Being a Christian is doing the same truth.

It is not surprising, then, that the writings of Karl Rahner abound with books of sermons, prayers and meditations along with his more theological investigations. For him the former were not pious ornaments, mere icing on the substantial cake of his theology, but were an essential part of doing theology. As he puts it in one of his interviews:

I would say that I have always done theology with a view to kerygma, preaching, pastoral care. For that reason, I have written relatively many books on devotion in the standard sense such as the book *On Prayer* and *Watch and Pray with Me* ...[44]

For Karl Rahner theology must not just talk about God, but must introduce people to the experience of those realities from out of which talk about God emerges. He calls this process of introduction

28

'mystagogy',[45] a strange-sounding mediaeval term, but its meaning is clear. It is the process of learning what faith and theology mean from within one's own existence and experience, and not merely by indoctrination from without. It is only when one is in touch with the realities that theology is talking about that one can really see what theology means. Hence Rahner quotes with approval the remark of Hans Urs von Balthasar that part of theology must be done 'on one's knees'.[46]

Nor is it surprising that late in life he was to say and mean that the 'spirituality of Ignatius, learned through the practice of prayer', was more significant for him 'than all learned philosophy and theology inside and outside the Order'.[47] For the *Spiritual Exercises* of St Ignatius are designed to put one in touch with the mysteries of the life of Jesus, to impart not abstract knowledge, but concrete realization of the truth. It was here that Rahner had his own 'mystagogical' introduction to theology and the encounter with Jesus of Nazareth that he says is the starting point of theology. Here, too, he learned the incarnational principle of 'finding God in all things' that was to influence his theology in many ways.

Faith and theology, then, do not begin with philosophy, but with an encounter with Jesus of Nazareth. For Rahner, nevertheless, philosophy can and should play an important role in the elaboration of theology. We turn now to examine that role in his theology and the particular philosophy he found most helpful.

Notes

1   SW appeared in 1939 and HW in 1941; see Chapter 1, notes 9 and 10.

2   'The human question of meaning in face of the absolute mystery of God', TI 18, pp. 89–104.

3   Ibid., p. 95.

4   Ibid., p. 97.

5   FC, p. 22.

6   Ibid., p. 32.

7   'Philosophy and philosophizing in theology', TI 9, p. 56.

8   Ibid.

9   'The hiddenness of God', TI 16, p. 238.

10   Ibid., p. 231.

11   Ibid.

12　See, for example, the teaching of Leo the Great (DS 294), Pope Martin I (DS 501), the Fourth Lateran Council in 1215 (DS 800, 804) and the First Vatican Council in 1870 (DS 3001).

13　'The human question of meaning', pp. 91–2.

14　Ibid., p. 92. See also Rahner's lengthy treatment of God's incomprehensibility in 'The concept of mystery in Catholic theology', TI 4, pp. 36–73; and his study of the question in Thomas Aquinas, 'An investigation of the incomprehensibility of God in St Thomas Aquinas', TI 16, pp. 244–54.

15　'The human question of meaning', p. 93.

16　'On the current relationship between philosophy and theology', TI 13, p. 61.

17　FC, p. 177.

18　This is explained and developed in FC, pp. 305–11, and pp. 203–6. The term 'existentiell' must be distinguished from 'existential'. An 'existential' is a constitutive aspect or dimension of our human existence, something which is part of our concrete human nature prior to the exercise of our freedom. 'Existentiell', on the other hand, refers to the free, personal appropriation and realization of something as distinguished from knowing about it only theoretically or in abstract concepts. 'Existentiell Christology', then, is a personal relationship to and knowledge of Jesus as distinguished from knowing doctrines about him.

19　FC, p. 1.

20　'The hiddenness of God', pp. 240–1.

21　Ibid., p. 241. Rahner refers here to his lengthy treatment of this question in 'Dogmatic reflections on the knowledge and self-consciousness of Christ', TI 5, pp. 193–215, which we will be treating in Chapter 4.

22　'On the theology of hope', TI 10, p. 250.

23　Ibid.

24　Ibid., p. 255.

25　Ibid.

26　Ibid., p. 251.

27　'Reflections on the unity of the love of neighbour and the love of God', TI 6, p. 233.

28　'The human question of meaning', p. 100.

29　'The hiddenness of God', p. 233.

30　Ibid.

31　'The human question of meaning', pp. 99–100. See also 'The hiddenness of God', pp. 233–4.

32　'The human question of meaning', p. 101.

33   See 'The "commandment" of love in relation to the other command-
     ments', TI 5, pp. 439-59.

34   FC, pp. 309-10.

35   'Reflections on the unity', pp. 233-4.

36   Ibid., p. 234.

37   Ibid.

38   Ibid., p. 235.

39   Ibid., p. 247.

40   'On the theology of hope', p. 256.

41   Ibid., p. 257.

42   Ibid.

43   Ibid., pp. 250, 256-7. See also 'The Ignatian mysticism of joy in the
     world', TI 3, pp. 277-93.

44   *Karl Rahner in Dialogue*, p. 256.

45   See, for example, 'Theology and the arts', *Thought* LVII, no. 224
     (March 1982), p. 26.

46   Ibid., p. 25.

47   *Karl Rahner in Dialogue*, p. 191.

3

Grace and nature

In one of his many discussions of the hiddenness of God, Karl Rahner makes the following comment on his use of philosophy:

> The following reflections may seem philosophical and speculative, but in fact they proceed from a conviction of faith, that is, from a strictly theological proposition.[1]

This statement, made in the specific context of God's hiddenness, contains the key for understanding Rahner's use of philosophy in general. His philosophy proceeds from his theology in the sense that it provides concepts and language in which to clarify, explain and express the meaning of 'a conviction of faith'. Theology does not proceed from philosophy in the sense that the latter would be the source of faith's conviction. Faith and theology come first, but philosophy, though secondary, is essential to faith and theology because we must have 'the courage to think'[2] about our faith and show that it is reasonable and makes sense, that it is 'intrinsically worthy of belief'.[3] Otherwise faith becomes a blind leap into the darkness of a dogmatism either of the Bible or of Church teaching.[4] Perhaps the best way to gain an understanding and appreciation of Rahner's use of philosophy, then, is to see it at work in some of the theological contexts in which he employs it.

When the Jesuit theology faculty in Innsbruck was reconstituted after the Second World War and Rahner resumed his teaching there, Catholic theology was torn by a controversy between a movement in France known as the *nouvelle théologie* and Rome's swift and stern rejection of this 'new theology'. One of its leading proponents was Henri de Lubac, who published a major study in 1946 under the title *Surnaturel*.[5] Without mentioning de Lubac by name, Rome took issue with his understanding of the supernatural in 1950 with the publication of the encyclical *Humani Generis* by Pius XII. The issue was the relationship between grace and nature, and the problem was how the human desire for God could be truly human, that is, an intrinsic part of human nature, as de Lubac wanted it to be, and yet still be grace. For if it were a natural desire, was not the God who created human nature bound to satisfy it? If God were so bound, how could divine grace still be free? In the words of the encyclical:

> Others are destroying the true 'gratuity' of the supernatural order when they maintain that God cannot create beings endowed with intellect without ordering and calling them to the beatific vision.[6]

In the eyes of Rome the 'new theology' did not do justice to the sovereign freedom of God's grace.

Rahner saw that much was at stake in this seemingly abstruse theological dispute, and that it was therefore necessary to resolve the apparent dilemma in a way that did justice to Rome's concern and also to the legitimate concern of the 'new theology'. The latter criticized what Rahner calls the 'extrinsicism' of the average textbook's understanding of the relationship between grace and nature:

> Ultimately this amounts to the reproach of 'extrinsicism': grace appears there as a mere superstructure, very fine in itself certainly, which is imposed upon nature by God's decree, and in such a way that the relationship between the two is no more intense than that of a freedom from contradiction (of a 'potentia oboedientialis' understood purely negatively); nature does indeed acknowledge the end and means of the supernatural order (glory and grace) as in themselves the highest goods, but it is not clear why it 'should have much time for' these highest goods.[7]

In such an understanding, Rahner goes on to say, a free being 'could always reject such a good without thereby having *inwardly* the experience of losing its end'.[8]

Moreover, if the supernatural order of God's grace was indeed

33

free, as Pius XII and the whole Christian tradition taught, but was merely an extrinsic addition to human nature, 'a mere superstructure', as Rahner says, then the whole realm of the human as such seemed to be deprived of any ultimate meaning. Indeed, the whole order of God's natural creation would seem to be merely the stage whereon human beings worked out their supernatural salvation, and to have no ultimate meaning in itself. Likewise, human, secular history would seem but an empty charade wherein the drama of supernatural, salvation history, the only history that ultimately mattered, was played out.

What was at stake in Rome's dispute with the 'new theology', then, was anything but an innocuous theological subtlety. How one understands the relationship between grace and nature entails fundamental questions about the Church's theology of matter, its theology of creation and its theology of history. It also entails the question of the presence of God's grace outside the Judaeo-Christian tradition. All of these questions were to be addressed in varying degrees of explicitness fifteen years later in Vatican II's teaching on the relationship of the Church to the modern, secular world and to non-Christian religions. Rahner's work on the relationship of grace and nature was to help prepare the way for this teaching.

Pius XII, however, was still far removed from the teaching of Vatican II. It was rather the First Vatican Council that finds an echo in his teaching. Vatican I discussed the question of grace and nature in the specific context of knowledge when it asked how the natural knowledge of God is related to the supernatural knowledge of revelation. Its response stresses the difference between these two kinds of knowledge, and expresses their relationship in a negative way by saying that they cannot contradict each other because they both have the same source in God.[9] Rahner sees this response as not fully adequate because natural and graced knowledge, and therefore nature and grace in general, appear to be strangers for whom the best that can be hoped is a kind of peaceful coexistence.[10] Granted the distinction between grace and nature that Vatican I stressed, must there not also be a deeper unity within the creative and redemptive work of God?

Vatican II, on the other hand, in its Pastoral Constitution on the Church in the Modern World, discussed the question of grace and nature in the context not of knowledge, but of history. It asked how the salvation history in which the Church is involved is related to all of human history. It goes beyond Vatican I in affirming a positive relationship between these two histories when it says of the community of believers:

> United in Christ, they are led by the Holy Spirit in their journey to the kingdom of their Father and they have welcomed the news of salvation which is meant for every man. That is why this community realizes that it is truly and intimately linked with mankind and its history.[11]

Whatever the nature of this 'true and intimate link', it is more than merely a lack of opposition between the two histories. The Council likewise takes a positive view of the presence of grace and the possibility of salvation outside the Judaeo-Christian tradition.[12]

In all of these texts Vatican II maintains the absolute freedom and gratuity of God's grace, but at the same time wishes to see it as a universal possibility for every person. It gives as the reason for this the universal saving will of God

> 'who wishes all men to be saved and to come to the knowledge of the truth. For there is one God, and one Mediator between God and men, himself man, Christ Jesus, who gave himself a ransom for all' (1 Tim 2:4–5), 'neither is there salvation in any other' (Acts 4:12).[13]

Likewise, it wishes to see the history of grace in the world as 'truly and intimately linked' to all of human history. What concept of grace would allow it to be utterly free and gratuitous and at the same time an intrinsic part of all human history?

Rahner agrees with the 'new theology' that 'an extrinsicism of this kind has been current in the average teaching on grace in the last few centuries'.[14] He then goes on to show that God's will or God's decree to endow human beings with grace cannot be understood in a purely external or extrinsic way:

> On the contrary, *must* not what God decrees for man be *eo ipso* an interior ontological constituent of his concrete quiddity *'terminative'*, even if it is not a constituent of his 'nature'? For an ontology which grasps the truth that man's concrete quiddity depends utterly on God, is not his binding disposition *eo ipso* not just a juridical decree of God but precisely what man *is*, hence not just an imperative proceeding from God but man's most inward depths?[15]

35

Rahner maintains that such a divine decree necessarily entails an ontological change in human existence:

> If God gives creation and man above all a supernatural end and this end is first 'in intentione', then man (and the world) *is* by that very fact always and everywhere inwardly other in structure than he would be if he did not have this end, and hence other as well before he has reached this end partially (the grace which justifies) or wholly (the beatific vision).[16]

He disagrees, however, with the 'new theology' at one important point:

> But is this inner reference of man to grace a constituent of his 'nature' in such a way that the latter cannot be conceived without it, i.e., as pure nature, and hence such that the concept of *natura pura* becomes incapable of complete definition? It is at this point that we are bound to declare our inability to accept the view which has been attributed to the 'nouvelle théologie' and has met with so much opposition.[17]

In order to be able to conceive of nature without grace and thereby safeguard the gratuity of grace, Rahner proposes that grace be understood as a 'supernatural existential'.[18]

The term 'existential' was used by Martin Heidegger in his analysis of human existence to designate those components which were constitutive of human existence, that is, those features which were proper to and characteristic of a human existent and therefore distinguished a human being from other kinds of beings. If God created human beings in the first place so that there would be creatures with whom God could share his own divine life in knowledge and love, that is, if God created human beings precisely for the life of grace, then the offer and the possibility of grace is given with human nature itself as this nature has been historically constituted. Creation is intrinsically ordered to the supernatural life of grace as its deepest dynamism and final goal. The offer of this grace, then, is an existential, an intrinsic component of human existence and part of the very definition of the human in its historical existence.

But since God did not have to create human beings for this purpose and end, this existential is properly called a 'supernatural existential'. This means that it is part of human nature only because of God's free and gratuitous disposition of this nature. He could have created it otherwise, as what Rahner calls 'pure nature'. Created human existence is itself a free gift of God, and beyond this God freely bestows upon human beings the gift of himself in grace. However, since human beings must freely accept this gift if there is to be a personal relationship of knowledge and love with God, it is the *offer* and *possibility* of grace which in the first instance is an existential. Whether it is accepted or rejected is an entirely different question. This is a question not about human nature, but about human life and human history.

Rahner stresses, too, that the supernatural existential is not a 'thing' or a 'link' between nature and the supernatural order of grace.[19] To understand it this way, as explaining why nature has a certain affinity for grace, merely shifts the problem to explaining why nature has an affinity for the supernatural existential, and so it would solve nothing. It is rather the concrete mode in which human nature was created and actually exists as a result of God's intention in creating it. 'Pure nature' is an abstract possibility, not a reality. Hence as an explanatory term the supernatural existential wants to affirm something about the reality of grace, namely, that it is a constituent part of our historical human existence.

This affirmation carries many implications for our understanding of grace, both theoretical and practical, the latter of which will concern us in later chapters. First, the conjunction of the two terms 'supernatural' and 'existential' affirms that grace is utterly free and gratuitous and at the same time that it is utterly intrinsic to human nature and human existence, thus resolving the dilemma mentioned earlier. The offer of grace is part of being human, indeed, it is the deepest and innermost truth about the human. If grace is a supernatural existential, then, as Augustine said, 'God is closer to us than we are to ourselves', for he is there prior to the exercise of our freedom and summoning us to a response in freedom. Moreover, the 'us' of Augustine's statement is all of us, every human being who has ever existed or ever will exist in all times, places and cultures, people of all religions and people of no religion.[20] The offer of grace is universal because God 'wishes everyone to be saved and to come to the knowledge of the truth' (1 Tim 2:4).

But conceiving of God's gracious presence in human existence as an existential is to understand this presence as universal in a second and equally important sense. The term 'existential' does not denote something that is present here or there or now and then, but an aspect of human existence that is present and operative in all human affairs. An existential is a transcendental determination in the sense that it permeates and pervades all of human existence. The presence of God in grace is not confined to one compartment of human life or to particular times and places, but touches everything human. Hence Vatican II can say in its Pastoral Constitution on the Church in the Modern World that for the followers of Christ 'nothing genuinely human fails to raise an echo in their hearts'.[21] For everything genuinely human can be an echo of God and the occasion for encountering God's gracious presence.

Understood as an existential, then, grace is universal both in the sense of every human being and in the sense of everything human. This remains true even after the Fall and taking into account the fact of sin and the presence of evil in human life and human history. For in the Catholic understanding human nature, though wounded and weakened by sin, is not destroyed by it nor rendered totally corrupt. 'But where sin increased, grace abounded all the more', as Paul said (Rom 5:20). For the power of God's love and grace is stronger than the power of sin and cannot be conquered by it. The presence of grace is not eradicated by the presence of evil, but remains an ever-present existential of human existence.

A further reflection of Rahner on the scholastic notions of 'created' and 'uncreated' grace brings out another and equally important point in his understanding of grace. He points out that the Pauline theology of grace stresses that grace means primarily the presence of the 'Holy Spirit', the personal Spirit of God, who 'is given to us' and 'dwells within us'.[22] John, too, speaks of Christ 'abiding in us', of the Father and Son 'making their dwelling in us', and of the Spirit who has been given to us.[23] Likewise, the Fathers of the Church, especially the Greek Fathers, 'see the created gifts of grace as a *consequence* of God's substantial communication to justified men'.[24] Scholastic theology, on the other hand, has reversed this priority:

However diverse they may be among themselves, it is true of all the scholastic theories that they see God's indwelling and his conjunction with the justified man as based exclusively upon created grace. In virtue of the fact that created grace is imparted to the soul God imparts himself to it and dwells in it. Thus what we call uncreated grace (i.e., God as bestowing himself upon man) is a function of created grace.[25]

Rahner offers a way to return to the more personal and more immediately religious understanding of grace in Scripture and the Fathers by thinking of grace not just as a created effect of God's efficient causality, but, based on an analogy with the immediate presence of God in the beatific vision, as God's actual presence and indwelling through a mode of quasi-formal causality.[26] From this vantage point, then, the theory of the supernatural existential asserts that God in his own personal Spirit is present throughout all of history, and that human beings in all of their human encounters are also encountering God.

Rahner's use of the philosophical concept of an existential in his theology of grace is a good illustration of his understanding of the relationship of philosophy and theology. The starting point, as he said (see p. 32 above), is a 'conviction of faith', a 'strictly theological proposition'. In this instance the faith conviction is rooted in the scriptural assertion of God's universal saving will, and in the belief that if God truly wishes the salvation of all, then it must be a concrete possibility for everyone. One way, although obviously not the only way, of understanding grace as a universal possibility is to understand it as an existential in human life. Philosophy serves theology's task of seeking an understanding of faith in the sense in which Anselm defined theology as *fides quaerens intellectum*, faith seeking understanding.

Moreover, while the faith itself remains the same, different times and different concerns will require the use of different philosophies that give rise to different theological expressions of the faith. In modern times, for example, the discovery of whole continents of people untouched by the preaching of the Christian message, and the discovery that the history of the human race was incalculably longer than the few thousand years imagined in earlier ages, raised questions for theology that did not exist before. If God wishes all people to be saved, how does grace reach the vast multitudes of people who have existed before and beyond the reach of Christian preaching? They, indeed, constitute the vast majority of the human race, while those who have heard the Christian message are but a very small minority. How is God in his grace related to all of humanity?

Questions like this create the task for theology to understand God's universal saving will in a way that is plausible and credible in this new cultural situation. They give rise to different ways of conceiving God's gracious presence in the world and provide the impetus for Rahner to understand this presence as a supernatural existential. For then this presence is as universal as God's saving will itself, and salvation becomes a concrete possibility for everyone. It is not confined to particular times and places and to a small minority of the human race. In this way the philosophical concept can help theology express Christian faith in a more universal and less particularistic, exclusivistic way. Understanding God's gracious presence as a supernatural existential provides one theological way to express the Second Vatican Council's optimistic view of the possibility of salvation for all peoples.

But as is often the case, solving one theological problem creates further problems, or at least leaves other problems unsolved. In this instance there remains the question of how grace is to be understood so as to include the notion of revelation, thereby creating the possibility of faith as a personal response to revelation. These is also the question of how revelation remains a genuine historical reality, as it has been understood in the Judaeo-Christian tradition, and does not become merely some kind of unhistorical, interior illumination. Rahner addresses both of these questions.

If, first of all, the history of grace and salvation in the world is coextensive with all of human history, though not identical with it because history also includes the rejection of grace and salvation, then the history of God's revelation must also be coextensive with all of history:

> But anyone who as a good Thomist holds fast to the principle that the supernatural gratuitous elevation of man by the grace of salvation (whether accepted or rejected) is an elevation to a new formal object of the spirit which is unattainable by any merely natural act—i.e., an elevation to a new, even though perhaps permanently unthematic horizon, within which all spiritual existence takes place—cannot really deny that the universal salvation history that is co-existent in space and time with world history signifies also in a true sense a coextensive, universal *history of revelation*, if it is permissible to give the name of revelation even to the simple opening out of an *absolute* horizon of spiritual existence by the free act of God's self-communication.[27]

The claim that a universal history of grace entails a universal history of revelation is based on Rahner's understanding of the nature of human knowledge, which provides another instance of his use of philosophy in the service of theology's search for an understanding of the faith.

Commenting on our usual understanding of knowledge, Rahner observes:

> We often imagine the essential nature of knowledge after the model of a tablet on which an object is inscribed, whereby the object comes from outside, as it were, and appears on the tablet. We imagine knowledge after the likeness of a mirror in which some object or other is reflected.[28]

This is the 'image' or 'copy' theory of knowledge taken for granted by what is called 'naive realism', the notion that knowledge is simply looking at what is out there. There is indeed a receptive element in knowledge, a being determined by the reality we encounter, but this is not the whole story. For 'in reality', says Rahner, 'knowledge has a much more complex structure'.[29]

For when being reaches that degree of intensity and interiority possessed by human beings it becomes present to itself and conscious of itself. The very mode of being of human beings is a mode of knowledge, that mode of knowledge which Rahner calls 'self-presence'. To exist at this level of being which includes self-presence is to exist as spirit, and in spiritual beings knowledge and being are identical. Their being is self-presence. This identity is realized perfectly in God who is pure spirit, and imperfectly in human beings because they are also material.[30] They are spirit embodied in matter, and hence the 'complex structure' of their knowledge. The 'image' or 'copy' theory of knowledge neglects the spiritual element of self-presence and models knowledge exclusively on materiality and sense knowledge.

Whenever, therefore, as material beings we encounter a reality through the senses as the object of our knowledge, as spiritual beings we are simultaneously self-present and aware of ourselves as knowing. Our awareness of our knowledge encompasses both poles of the single knowledge relationship, both the known object and ourselves as the knowing subject. In this sense our knowledge is always bipolar: whenever we are present to another as the object of our knowledge we are simultaneously present to ourselves. This does not mean that there are two objects of the knowledge, for this self-presence is not like knowing an object, but is the 'luminous realm' within which the single object we are attending to and focusing on can 'become manifest'.[31] To use a simple and limping analogy, if the objective pole of knowledge is like something illuminated by a beam of light, the self-presence of the knower is like a burning and luminous coal that is the source of light. We can, of course, make ourselves the object of our knowledge when we think about ourselves in an act of introspection, but that is not the primary, unthematic kind of self-presence that is being described here.

Students of Thomas Aquinas will recognize in this description a variety of Thomistic themes in non-Thomistic garb. The passive, receptive element in knowledge in which we are determined by the reality we encounter through the senses is what Thomas calls the 'possible intellect' or the intellect as a potency. The active, illuminating aspect of knowledge is the 'agent intellect' or the intellect as active in the process of knowledge. The fact that all of our knowledge occurs in an encounter with objective reality through the senses and is not derived from 'innate ideas' is what Thomas calls the 'conversion to the phantasm' which necessarily accompanies all knowledge. The self-presence which accompanies this objective knowledge is what Thomas calls the *reditio completa in seipsum*, the complete return of the knowing subject to itself in knowing an object. The 'conversion' is the *a posteriori* factor in knowledge, and the 'return' or the self-presence is the *a priori* factor. Both factors are always simultaneously present in all of our knowledge.[32]

One can also recognize the influence of Pierre Rousselot and Joseph Maréchal in Rahner's interpretation of Thomas Aquinas, the interpretation which has come to be known as 'transcendental Thomism'.[33] In transcendental philosophy the knowing subject becomes the focus of inquiry and investigation in what has been described as the 'turn to the subject'. For Rahner this interest in or turn to the subject did not mean a turning away from or a lessening of interest in the object. Rather, while continuing to insist on the objectivity of knowledge and its mediation through the senses, on the element of *a posteriori* 'realism' in Aquinas, he also wanted to do justice to the subjective and *a priori* element whose roots he also found in Thomas, but which were further developed in transcendental philosophy.

Failure to take account of the self-presence and active role of the knower in knowledge leads to the naive realism of the 'image' or 'copy' theory of knowledge. On the other hand, neglecting the basis of all knowledge in our sense experience of the real world leads to some form of subjectivism or idealism. By reading Thomas in the light of these later insights of transcendental philosophy and allowing each tradition to enrich the other, Rahner found a more adequate theory of knowledge than that available in the usual scholastic interpretation of Aquinas. More importantly for his purposes, he found a theory of more value for theology.

For, again with Maréchal, he finds in the self-presence of the human knower not a static presence, but an openness and a dynamism, a drive or a desire that reaches out beyond the actual object known to a larger horizon, indeed, an unlimited horizon.[34] The world of our experience and our sense intuition, the thematic content of our knowledge, is always encompassed by this larger horizon of which we are also aware and which forms the unthematic content of our knowledge. *Within* our experience of the world, then, and as an aspect of this experience, we are already beyond it and in touch with more than the world of sensible realities. This 'beyond' and this 'more', says Rahner, are what Thomas means by the *excessus* in our knowledge: we are in the world, but because we are spirit in the world and in history, we are not enclosed within the world nor confined within the historical present, but open to its future. In the single experience, then, we are simultaneously present to and in touch with the world of objective realities, with ourselves as knowers and with this larger, unlimited horizon in what Rahner calls the transcendental element in our experience.[35]

This formal analysis of the structure of human knowing says nothing, of course, about the concrete content of our knowledge, but it does provide Rahner with a language in which to talk about this content. To those who deny the possibility of knowing God, or the possibility of receiving a revelation from God, or the possibility of knowing anything other than the empirical data of experience, Rahner points to the rich and multi-dimensional nature of our experience to establish all of these possibilities. He wants to show that when faith and theology speak of God and his revelation, its language has meaning in the context of our experience and makes sense in that context. Whether it is also true is a matter of history, not philosophy. But because human beings are *spirit* in world and in history, they are possible subjects of an encounter with God's word in history.

Rahner found in transcendental Thomism, then, a language in which he could do theology with intellectual rigour and honesty in the world of modern critical philosophy and modern empirical science. In this world, too, God-talk makes sense and can point to its roots in experience. But its idiom and its grammar are different from scholastic forms of Thomism. For its approach to God is always through the world of our objective, historical experience and as an element *within* that experience. God, however, is not encountered as one object among others in that world, but as the deepest dimension of all our encounters:

> Hence the original knowledge of God is not the kind of knowledge in which one grasps an object which happens to present itself directly or indirectly from outside. It has rather the character of a transcendental experience. Insofar as this subjective, non-objective luminosity of the subject in its transcendence is always orientated towards the holy mystery, the knowledge of God is always present unthematically and without name, and not just when we begin to speak of it.[36]

The speaking and the naming, of course, that is, the interpretation of this experience, are derived by Rahner from his Christian tradition. What his philosophical analysis allows him to do is connect this tradition with the experience of people today and help them to understand what the tradition is saying. The task of theology, as Anselm said, is always one of seeking an *understanding* of the faith.

Making this connection between Christian tradition and our own experience is what Rahner calls the very important 'mystagogical' task of theology. This task includes two movements or directions. Theology must help those who have been shaped and formed by the language of Christian tradition, who have been educated and 'indoctrinated' into it from without, to discover from within their own experience what the language really means. Its terms and concepts must be driven back 'to that original knowledge, to that original experience in which what is meant and the experience of what is meant are still one'.[37] One really knows what statements about God's love or God's forgiveness mean when one has experienced the reality they are talking about. Secondly, theology must find the concepts and language that can objectify and express the experience in a way that can keep the tradition alive today.[38] It is here that philosophy can be of help in theology's task.

By 'turning to the subject' with modern philosophy, then,

Rahner has arrived at an understanding of human existence and human knowledge which allows him to say that the presence of God's grace is also the presence of God's revelation, that a universal history of grace is also and necessarily a universal history of revelation and a universal possibility of faith. Whatever affects the being of human beings in themselves also affects their knowledge. Hence Rahner could say in the earlier citation that no good Thomist could doubt that the supernatural elevation of man's being in grace was also the elevation of his knowledge to a 'new formal object' or a 'new horizon' unattainable by any merely natural act. As the horizon of every person's entire existence, God's self-communication as grace and revelation are present at least unthematically in all human knowledge and freedom, and are accepted or rejected in all human choices.

But as was said earlier, Rahner's turn to the subject was not a turning away from the world of objects. This is the abiding Thomistic element in his transcendental Thomism that distinguishes it from any form of subjectivism or idealism. The self-presence of human knowledge and freedom, and therein the presence of their unlimited horizon, takes place only in the process of knowing and choosing within the world of historical realities. One becomes present to oneself only in the process of becoming present to another. Transcendence, then, is not a springboard out of the world and out of history, but a way of existing in them. It is being in the world and history as spirit and as freedom. Indeed, it is in the human spirit that matter reaches the level of self-presence and freedom that makes human history possible.[39]

One can speak, therefore, of the transcendental element in revelation. It refers to what Rahner calls the 'new formal object' or the 'new horizon' within which we exist. But there can be no formal object without a material object nor a horizon without the content for which it is the horizon. Hence there can be no such thing as transcendental revelation by itself, but only as an element in our historical experience. Human beings are always transcendence within history, always spirit in world. Transcendental revelation, therefore, is not a purely interior illumination freeing one from the particularities of history, including the particular history of the Judaeo-Christian tradition. It always takes place within and as a dimension of our encounter with historical realities.[40]

We have examined two theological contexts in which Karl Rahner employs philosophy in his search for an understanding of a 'conviction of faith'.[41] He uses the Heideggerian notion of an existential to explain his faith conviction that God's gracious presence is an intrinsic and universal dimension of all human existence while maintaining the absolute gratuity of this presence. He uses the understanding of knowledge and being elaborated in transcendental Thomism to explain his faith conviction that, though all human knowledge is rooted in the senses, human beings can know God; and though all human existence is existence in relationship to the world and to history, human beings through grace can be personally related to God in knowledge and love. These faith convictions themselves are rooted not in philosophy but in history, most especially in the history of Jesus of Nazareth. To that history we now turn.

Notes

1 'The hiddenness of God', TI 16, p. 235.

2 'Philosophy and philosophizing in theology', TI 9, p. 63.

3 Ibid., p. 52.

4 Ibid., pp. 48–52. See also 'Philosophy and theology', TI 6, pp. 71–81, and 'On the current relationship between philosophy and theology', TI 13, pp. 61–79.

5 Henri de Lubac, *Surnaturel. Études historiques* (Paris: Aubier, 1946).

6 DS 3891.

7 'Concerning the relationship between nature and grace', TI 1, p. 298.

8 Ibid.

9 DS 3015–3017.

10 'Philosophy and theology', pp. 72–4.

11 GS, no. 1.

12 GS, no. 22. After saying that 'grace works in an unseen way' in the hearts of all people of good will, the Council continues: 'For, since Christ died for all men, and since the ultimate vocation of man is in fact one, and divine, we ought to believe that the Holy Spirit in a manner known only to God offers to every man the possibility of being associated with this paschal mystery'. See also LG, no. 16 and AG, no. 7.

13 AG, no. 7.

14 'Concerning the relationship between nature and grace', p. 298.

15 Ibid., p. 302.

16 Ibid., pp. 302–3.

17 Ibid., p. 303.

18 Ibid., p. 302, note 1.

19 Ibid.

20 See 'History of the world and salvation history', TI 5, pp. 97–114; 'Christianity and the non-Christian religions', TI 5, pp. 115–34; and FC, pp. 142–52.

21 GS, no. 1.

22 'Some implications of the scholastic concept of uncreated grace', TI 1, pp. 320–2.

23 Ibid., p. 322.

24 Ibid.

25 Ibid., p. 324.

26 Ibid., pp. 334ff.

27 'Philosophy and theology', p. 77.

28 FC, p. 17.

29 Ibid.

30 See SW, pp. 67–71. As Rahner puts it: 'Knowing is the being-present-to-itself of being, and this being-present-to-itself is the being of the existent' (p. 69). See also HW, pp. 38–43, and Rahner's summary of his epistemology in FC, pp. 14–23.

31 FC, p. 18.

32 Rahner's *Spirit in the World* is an analysis of Aquinas's metaphysics of knowledge seen in the light of modern transcendental and existential philosophy. All these themes are treated in detail there.

33 See SW, p. xlvii.

34 FC, pp. 19–20.

35 Ibid., pp. 20–1.

36 Ibid., p. 21.

37 Ibid., pp. 16–17.

38 Ibid., p. 16.

39 See Rahner's explanation of 'the historical mediation of transcendentality and transcendence' in FC, pp. 140–2.

40 Having shown in *Spirit in the World* that human beings *can* know God, it is the burden of Rahner's *Hearers of the Word* to show that it is to history that they must turn to listen for an actual word of God.

41 Rahner cautions, however, that there can be no 'pure philosophy' since there is no such thing as 'pure human nature': 'In his thinking man as a philosopher is in fact constantly subject to a theological *a priori*, namely that transcendental determination which orients him towards the immediate presence of God'. See 'On the current relationship between philosophy and theology', p. 63.

4

Jesus of Nazareth

If all theological reflection, including its use of philosophy, is rooted in faith as that for which it is seeking understanding and justification, faith itself is rooted in an encounter with historical reality. Rahner specifies what this reality is for Christian theology:

> In giving a justification for our faith in Christ, the basic and decisive point of departure, of course, lies in an encounter with the historical Jesus of Nazareth, and hence in an 'ascending Christology'.[1]

For Christian faith is not about eternal, necessary truths, but about something it affirms happened freely in history.

Since this encounter with history is a faith encounter, Rahner poses the question 'Is my faith that Jesus is the Christ legitimate?', rather than asking the 'objective' question 'Is Jesus the Christ?' He does this in order to stress that the identification of Jesus as the Christ is a free affirmation in faith. But this does not exclude or minimize the 'objective' question, for it is included in the structure of faith:

> Because of this structure, precisely what is most 'objective' is disclosed only to the most radical subjective act, and at the same time precisely the 'subjective act' knows itself to be empowered and justified by the objective facts.[2]

In this chapter, then, we shall consider both the historical Jesus of Nazareth and the logic of faith's affirmations about him.

Because of the difficulties raised by modern historical criticism about the historical Jesus, Rahner finds that an approach other than his is prevalent today. It is an approach which tends to emancipate the beliefs of Christian faith from history. But a faith in Christ which is not rooted in the actual historical life of Jesus is a contemporary form of fideism:

> For today it is the fashion to be fideist so far as the Christian faith is concerned and more or less schizophrenic so far as the relationship between faith and reason (taken in a philosophical and historical sense) is concerned.[3]

Against this tendency Rahner states what he considers to be a fundamental thesis of Catholic theology:

> Catholic faith and its dogmatics as they have been understood up to now, and also as they will have to be understood in the future, remain indissolubly bound up not only with the historical existence of Jesus of Nazareth, but also with the historical events of a specific kind which took place during his life.[4]

Rahner affirms this indissoluble link between faith and history for several reasons.

From a theological point of view, the tendency to minimize or eliminate the importance of history is a gnostic tendency which manifested itself in the early Church in the heresy of Docetism. For the Docetists the historical, human life of Jesus was an appearance, not a reality. What was of importance was the divine reality or the divine truth that appeared behind this historical facade. Faith, then, was a deliverance from a history that was hostile or at best indifferent to religious reality and religious truth. The Church's response to this misinterpretation of Christian faith is found already in the Prologue to John's gospel with its insistence that the 'Word became flesh', and hence actually entered into the materiality of human history. Rahner concludes that the 'genuine Christianity of the New Testament' knew that its faith 'was related to a definite historical event', and that 'it did not simply posit this event or create it in faith', but rather 'receives its justification and foundation from this event'.[5]

The same point can be made for anthropological as well as theological reasons. It is impossible to think of genuine Christian faith unrelated to history, because all of our knowledge, including our knowledge of God, is mediated by history:

> However one might interpret transcendentality and existentiality more exactly, and make them the real ground of his faith, we cannot *in principle* possess them without a reference to real history.[6]

From this vantage point, too, Christian faith, precisely as faith in God, cannot escape the 'burden of history', but must be grounded in the historical Jesus of Nazareth. For what Christian faith affirms is that in him God has entered into time and history.

In maintaining so uncompromisingly the intrinsic connection of faith and history, Rahner does not ignore or minimize the difficulties posed by modern historical research which are what give rise to the flight to fideism. He accepts the conclusions of contemporary exegesis that the books of the New Testament, including the gospels, were not intended to be history in our sense, nor to give us a biography or a life of Jesus, but are proclamations of faith in Jesus.[7] They were written from the vantage point of resurrection faith and present theological interpretations or theological portraits of Jesus. The interpretations and the portraits vary from writer to writer, and give evidence of very early theological developments in the Christian communities dating even from before the earliest writings of the New Testament. Nevertheless, this faith and this theology were 'related to a definite historical event', and Christian faith today must continue to maintain the ' "substantial" historicity' of the gospel narratives.[8]

Culling his material from what he considers reliable exegetical sources, Rahner summarizes this ' "substantial" historicity' in broad strokes.[9] Jesus lived in and was part of the Jewish religious milieu of his people and in general accepted it as legitimate and willed by God. He took part in their religious life which included temple and synagogue, laws and customs, holy scriptures, priests and teachers. In this sense his message was one of religious reform rather than of radical religious revolution. It was, however, a radical religious reform that he preached. He broke the absolute lordship of the law which had usurped the place of God and fought against the legalism which sought justification by works.

He lived with a sense of radical closeness to God as the ultimate reality who was simply taken for granted as part of his life. It was for this reason that he befriended and saw himself in solidarity with social and religious outcasts, because his 'Father' loved them. His radical preaching and exhortation to reform were a call to conversion because the kingdom of God was 'at hand' (Mark 1:14-15). He intended to gather disciples, whom he called to 'follow' him. While accepting the struggle which this attitude and his activity provoked on the part of the religious and social establishment, he was not a social critic in the modern, sociological sense. At first he hoped for the success of his religious mission in the sense of the 'conversion' of his people, but in time saw this mission bringing him into mortal conflict with the religious and political society. But he faced his death resolutely and accepted it at least as the inevitable consequence of fidelity to the mission given him by God.

While Rahner questions the notion of miracle as an interruption of the laws of nature and sees miracles in the religious context of sign and call, he concludes that 'mighty deeds, signs and wonders' were part of the historical life of Jesus, because of the preponderance of the evidence.[10] But many questions about the pre-resurrection Jesus remain open in all this historical material. For example, did Jesus have a verbalized messianic consciousness about himself, and of the many titles applied to Jesus in the New Testament, which correspond most nearly to his own self-understanding? Did Jesus explicitly ascribe a saving function to his death beyond what was said above about his acceptance of it as the inevitable consequence of fidelity to his mission? Did Jesus foresee and intend the formation of his disciples into a new community, the community of the new Israel? The answers to all these questions were once thought to be easily available in a straightforward reading of the gospels as historical narratives. But today the situation is much more complex and ambiguous.

Much of this complexity and ambiguity revolves around the question of the knowledge and self-consciousness of Jesus in his earthly life. Because of his divine nature, the Tradition thought of Jesus as being in possession of the beatific vision during his earthly life, and therefore as having perfect knowledge of all things including his own identity. Indeed, his knowledge was such that faith or hope would have been superfluous in his life. This image of the earthly Jesus stands in stark contrast to the gospel portraits of him as questioning, doubting, learning, being surprised and even suffering the experience of being forsaken by God during his passion.

To account for this discrepancy Rahner distinguishes between a pre-conceptual and unthematic level of knowledge which is given with spiritual existence itself as its own self-presence, and that level of knowledge in which through interaction with the world of our experience we objectify and verbalize our knowledge. Jesus' union with God as a spiritual union included the former kind of knowledge, but this does not rule out, but rather requires, that his life, like that of every human being, was a life of learning and discovery through his historical experience. On this thematic level of knowledge it can be very difficult to ascertain from the gospel narratives how Jesus understood himself and his mission.[11]

Given the complexity and historical ambiguity of the gospel narratives, what in Rahner's view constitutes the minimum knowledge of Jesus that is both historically credible and keeps our faith rooted in and justified by the historical Jesus of Nazareth? He summarizes this knowledge in two theses:

> First, Jesus saw himself not merely as one among many prophets who in principle form an unfinished line which is always open towards the future, but understood himself rather as the *eschatological* prophet, as the absolute and definitive saviour, although the more precise question what a definitive saviour means and does not mean requires further reflection.[12]

The second thesis concerns what is necessary for this 'claim' of Jesus to be credible:

> Secondly, this claim of Jesus is credible for us when, from the perspective of our transcendental experience in grace of the absolute self-communication of the holy God, we look in faith to that event which mediates the saviour in his total reality: the resurrection of Jesus ... All other assertions about Jesus as the Christ can be left to faith itself as the content of faith.[13]

The assertions in these two theses, while they too form part of the content of our faith, are also grounds of our faith.

Before looking at how Rahner understands the relation between 'content' and 'ground' of faith, it is important to note a question he raises with regard to the assertion about Jesus' self-understanding in thesis one. Given the fact that the question about the self-understanding of the pre-Easter Jesus, in so far as this is still historically accessible to us, gives rise to very difficult and disputed problems, is it not perhaps possible to take the experience in faith of the resurrection of Jesus as the sole basis and ground of the development of the Church's faith in Jesus?[14] He raises this merely as a question which requires further reflection, but an eventual affirmative answer would affect how the resurrection is to be understood as a vindication of the historical life of Jesus.

However this might be decided, it remains true in either case that in addition to the historical events that engendered the faith of the first disciples, Scripture also speaks of the role of the Holy Spirit in their assent of faith. Rahner sees the relationship between the historical events and the grace of the Holy Spirit, which he interprets as the openness and dynamism of the human spirit towards God through the communication of God's Spirit, as one of mutual conditioning: the grace of faith opens one's eyes to the credibility of particular historical events, and these events themselves are the legitimate, objective justification for one's free assent in faith.[15] The importance of this reciprocal relationship is brought out in the distinction between the two senses of the word 'history'.[16]

There is a sense of history which refers merely to what actually happened in the past insofar as we can reconstruct what took place. There is another sense of history in which the events of the past, besides the fact that they actually took place, bear a further significance in some field of meaning or framework of reference. For example, Caesar's crossing of the Rubicon had a political significance for Rome that is of great importance to those interested in the political fortunes of Rome, whereas other facts about that day, for example, what Caesar had for breakfast, do not have such significance, except perhaps for someone interested in the eating habits of ancient Romans.

Our interests provide a subjective framework or context within which what happened in the past (history in the first sense) becomes meaningful and significant for us, becomes an historic event (history in the second sense). This is an example of what Rahner meant in the last chapter by the active, interpretative role of the knower in all of our objective knowledge of the real world and of real history. Everything we can know about what happened in the past is history in the first sense, but what one discovers or does not discover in the events of the past in the second sense of history depends partially on what one is looking for. It is in this sense, the Catholic tradition has always taught, that faith is a *free* act, and not merely a conclusion drawn from historical research or philosophical reasoning:

> This is not a sad and regrettable calamity for faith, but rather it follows from the very nature of faith because and insofar as it is a total and existentiell decision in freedom. Faith, therefore, can reach that by which it is grounded and borne only in this freedom, that is, in the act of faith itself.[17]

This is as true for the first believers in Jesus as it is for us today.

When, therefore, we say that the four gospels are not merely history books, but books of faith, we are pointing to the framework within which the first disciples of Jesus experienced his historical existence and recorded what they discovered there in the gospel narratives. It was the religious framework of Jewish faith and hope within which they discovered the historical and religious significance of his life. Likewise, when Rahner speaks of the relationship of 'mutual conditioning' between particular historical events in the life of Jesus and the 'eyes of faith' which see their credibility, he is pointing to the religious framework within which a Christian today discovers the reality and significance of Jesus for his or her life. Because of this reciprocal relationship the events are both the 'object' and the historical 'ground' of faith. Hence Rahner concludes:

> Salvation history strictly as such must belong to the dimension which we call the history of man in a very objective and real sense, and it is also affirmed as real and objective in the assertion in which faith grasps its object and its ground together in a free act and decision borne by grace.[18]

A non-believer who does not make this affirmation is not for this reason more objective or more historical. For as Rahner said above about this mutual relationship and the structure of faith:

> Because of this structure, precisely what is 'most objective' is disclosed only to the most radical subjective act, and at the same time

precisely the 'subjective act' knows itself to be empowered and justified by the objective facts.[19]

The relationship of faith to history as Rahner understands it, then, is not that faith adds more facts about Jesus than history can know, or fills in the gaps of our historical knowledge. Faith and history are qualitatively different moments in our relationship to the historical world. Faith sees meaning and significance in the data which history provides, and sees it in an act of recognition of that for which it had been searching. All knowledge is borne by desire and is the fruit of searching, so that Rahner observes:

> Even the most profane historical reality is not really given unless it is recognized. This brings it under the law of subjective apriority without which nothing at all can be known.[20]

The 'eyes of faith' which recognize Christ in the historical Jesus of Nazareth are but one form of this 'subjective apriority' or horizon of interest which characterizes all of our knowledge.

'Recognition' is a recurrent theme in the New Testament resurrection narratives which portray the faith of the first disciples in the risen Jesus as a process of 'recognizing' him.[21] Rahner sees the resurrection narratives as the pre-eminent New Testament material for grounding our faith today. The resurrection of Jesus, however, must be understood as intrinsically related to the whole life and death of Jesus which preceded it, and his life and death must be understood as intrinsically related to the resurrection:

> From this perspective, if the fate of Jesus has any soteriological significance at all, this significance can be situated neither in the death nor in the resurrection taken separately, but can only be illuminated now from the one and now from the other aspect of this single event.[22]

Beginning with the resurrection, therefore, he develops a single theology of the death and resurrection of Jesus as the final and culminating moment of his historical life.[23]

Before looking to what he calls 'the core of that original experience of Jesus as the Christ' in the resurrection, Rahner asks what are the intellectual presuppositions of such an experience.[24] First, as distinguished from the notion of the resuscitation of the dead in the Old and New Testaments, the resurrection of Jesus does not mean the resuscitation of his corpse, a 'coming back' to life:

> It means rather and precisely the permanent, redeemed, final and definitive validity of the single and unique life of Jesus who achieved the permanent and final validity of his life precisely through his death in freedom and obedience.[25]

Resurrection does not mean the (in terms of salvation) neutral survival of human existence, but the salvation of his concrete existence by God and in the presence of God, and the abiding, permanent validity of his history.

Moreover, this does not mean merely the survival of Jesus' 'cause' in the sense of what he was dedicated to, or the survival of an 'idea' which remains alive in his followers, but the survival of his person. This remains true however little we are able to imagine the 'how' of this final, 'eschatological' existence. For 'afterlife' or 'eternity' does not mean a further and unlimited extension or continuation of time after death, but entrance into a new mode of existence beyond time. In this sense eternity does not come 'after' death, but comes to be in time:

> In reality 'eternity' comes to be in time as its own mature fruit. Eternity does not really come 'beyond' the experienced time of our biological life in time and space and continue this time, but rather it subsumes time by being released from the time which *came to be* temporarily, and came to be so that the final and definitive could be done in freedom.[26]

Hence we cannot imagine what this non-temporal mode of existence is like or what the risen body of Jesus is like.

Rahner asserts that the horizon within which the first disciples were able to experience the risen Jesus in faith, and the horizon within which people today can still share the same experience in their faith, is what he calls 'transcendental hope in resurrection'.[27] By this he means that all human beings in their acts of freedom and responsibility necessarily desire that what they do makes some final sense, that it has some permanent meaning and validity, and that not everything is ultimately a matter of irrelevance and indifference. In this sense they experience the desire and hope for survival and resurrection, whether or not they are explicitly conscious of this implication of their acts of freedom and responsibility, and even if they reject this hope in an act of despair. This transcendental hope, then, is not a vague feeling or velleity that strikes a person now and again, but a necessary element in the process of accepting and affirming one's existence in freedom and responsibility. It is part of living as a free and responsible person.

Perhaps it is in the light of the experience of the resurrection of Jesus that we are able successfully to objectify and name this hope dimension of our own experience. Here too, then, the circle or the mutual dependence of the objective and subjective elements in our experience would be operative. Nevertheless, 'this transcendental hope in resurrection is the horizon of understanding for experiencing the resurrection of Jesus in faith'.[28] It grounds our search for the historical confirmation of this hope, and is the basis of our recognition and acceptance of the witness of others that Jesus is risen, that he lives. Therefore, while all successive generations of Christian believers are dependent on the first witnesses to the resurrection of Jesus as providing the ground of their faith, they do not stand entirely outside the experience of the apostolic witnesses as neutral or indifferent hearers of their witness. Rather they are interiorly disposed by their own hope to recognize the credibility of the first witnesses and to assent to it in faith.

Granted these presuppositions, what was the 'core' of the experience of the risen Jesus to which the first disciples give witness? Given the inconsistency and lack of harmony among the various gospel accounts of the appearances of the risen Jesus, it can be assumed that they are not literal descriptions of the experience itself, but secondary literary and dramatic embellishments of the original experience that 'Jesus is alive'. Of the original experience itself Rahner says:

> So far as the nature of this experience is accessible to us, it is to be explained after the manner of our experience of the powerful Spirit of the living Lord rather than in a way which either likens this experience too closely to mystical visions of an imaginative kind in later times, or understands it as an almost physical sense experience.[29]

This latter can hardly be the case since the risen Jesus was no longer part of the physical, sensible world.

The common thread that begins with this core experience and the simple confessional formula 'He is risen', and runs through all the texts that dramatize the Easter experience in a great variety of theological motifs, is the awareness that the experience is given to the disciples 'from without', and is not something they can produce. Jesus comes to them and appears to them. Moreover, it is the crucified Jesus as a quite definite individual with his very particular fate whom God has raised from the dead and thereby accepted and vindicated. While it is this experience which grounds and justifies their faith, at the same time it is in faith that they experience the risen Jesus, and it is only believers who do experience him. Hence it would be false to think of the resurrection as accessible to us 'historically' outside the faith of the first witnesses.

Rahner sees the vindication of Jesus and his claim in the resurrection as the starting point of all Christology. He explains this claim as:

> The claim that there is present with him a new and unsurpassable closeness of God which on its part will prevail victoriously and is inseparable from him. He calls this closeness the coming and the arrival of God's kingdom, which forces a person to decide explicitly whether or not he accepts this God who has come so close.[30]

It is at least implicit in this claim that Jesus is the last of the prophets or the 'eschatological prophet' of God's final word. It is the final word of God not because God arbitrarily decides not to say anything further, but because in offering *himself* in Jesus he leaves nothing further to be said. It is this new and radical immediacy of God that accounts for Jesus' breaking through the legalisms and rigidities of the law to the very presence of God himself.

This ascending Christology of the resurrection experience is the basis for the development of all the later Christologies of the New Testament and of the subsequent Councils of the Church. It is about Jesus that they wish to speak, and they try to bring to expression further implications about his person. Hence there is no opposition between the earlier, ascending, functional Christology and its later transposition into metaphysical and essential terms. If Jesus accomplished what the early Christology claims he did, then he must have been who the later Christology claims he was: the very son of God become flesh.

It is in light of the experience of the risen Jesus that the saving significance of the death of Jesus on the cross becomes manifest. Rahner says (see p. 52 above) about Jesus' own understanding of his death that he gave his life for others at least in the sense that he accepted his death as the inevitable consequence of fidelity to the mission given him by God. But at least in later New Testament Christology a redemptive significance is accorded to the death of Jesus: it removes human sinfulness before God and establishes a saving relationship between God and human beings. Moreover, Rahner continues:

> It cannot be said that according to the New Testament as a whole the death of Jesus merely convinces us of a forgiving and salvific will of God which is absolutely independent of this death. The death of Jesus is obviously regarded as a cause of our salvation in a true sense, but in what precise sense?[31]

In the New Testament this causality is understood among other ways as that of a sacrifice of his blood offered to God.

This understanding was a help in understanding the significance of the death of Jesus at the time because the idea of propitiating God through sacrifice was current at the time. But it is of little help today if we presume that the initiative in salvation comes from God, and sacrifices cannot be understood as producing a 'change' in God. Moreover, the connection between this idea and the experience of the risen Jesus is not altogether clear. It should be seen, then, as a secondary and derivative interpretation of this experience, although it was perfectly legitimate at the time.

Rahner suggests two approaches towards understanding the nature of this causality today. First, insofar as human history is a single history and the destiny of one person has significance for others, and insofar as God's saving will for all people was fully realized and accomplished in Jesus through the perfect response of his life and especially his total surrender to God in death, his life and death can be seen as the 'symbolic' or 'quasi-sacramental' cause of our salvation.[32] This means that the life, death and resurrection of Jesus is the sign or symbol in which God's saving will reaches its full and irrevocable realization and manifestation, and this event in the history of Jesus is a unique event in the common history of which we are all a part. The single history which we all share has already entered into eschatological salvation in the person and history of Jesus, who is thus the first moment and the inauguration of the final, eschatological stage of history for all of us.

Moreover, since the union with God achieved by Jesus' free and perfect reponse is the very end and goal for which God created the human race, the life, death and resurrection of Jesus can be seen as the final cause of our common human destiny.[33] What recommends these two types of causality is that they make clear that the causality exercised by the life, death and resurrection of Jesus for the salvation of all is the 'consequence' and not the 'cause' of God's gracious love and forgiveness.[34] As John expresses the divine initiative in his gospel, 'God so loved the world that he gave his only Son, that everyone who has faith in him may not die but have eternal life' (3:16).

John also expresses here the dimension of our relationship to Jesus of Nazareth which Rahner calls 'existentiell Christology'.[35] Since salvation is a personal union with God in knowledge and love, however much this union is the fruit of God's gracious initiative, and however much this union has been achieved in a unique way by Jesus through his life, death and resurrection as the symbolic and final cause of the salvation of the world, this union can become real for someone only through what John here calls 'faith', and to which Rahner would add hope and love. Existentiell Christology is the actual process of living in a relationship of faith, hope and love with Jesus of Nazareth wherein he is recognized and acknowledged as the true way to eternal life with God or to salvation. It is the 'encounter with the historical Jesus of Nazareth' which Rahner says (see p. 49 above) is the starting point of all Christology.

Christology as reflection on faith, then, is not primarily reflection on an idea about Jesus, but reflection on this lived faith relationship. For Christian faith is not primarily a theory about Jesus, but a praxis or a way of life. It is the life of discipleship in response to his call to 'follow' him. Rahner describes such a disciple as 'anyone who accepts Jesus as the ultimate truth about his life', or makes the 'law' of Jesus' life the law of one's own life.[36] It is by doing the truth that Jesus did that existentiell Christology acquires its concrete, experiential knowledge of Jesus of Nazareth. One sees here why Rahner accorded such importance to Ignatius Loyola and his *Spiritual Exercises* for his theology. Through the exercise not of the speculative intellect, but of the senses and the imagination, the *Exercises* are designed to put one 'in touch' with the actual Jesus and to give one a 'taste of' and a 'feel for' his life. In this encounter one does not 'grasp' something, but 'is grasped', and the faith which responds and follows is what Rahner calls the point of departure for all Christology.

Moreover, he says that all people at any point in human history, who in response to the movement of the Spirit, who is the Spirit of Jesus, do this same truth in their lives, are in touch with Jesus and know him by 'connaturality' on this existentiell level of knowledge, even though they have never heard of Jesus or learned doctrines about him. Such a person is living the life of what Rahner calls an 'anonymous Christian'.[37] It is in this sense that he interprets the assertion of Vatican II that the Holy Spirit offers to every person the possibility of being associated with the paschal mystery:[38]

> According to the Catholic understanding of the faith, as is clearly expressed in the Second Vatican Council, there can be no doubt that someone who has no concrete, historical contact with the explicit preaching of Christianity can nevertheless be a justified person who lives in the grace of Christ.[39]

For such a person is part of the same history of revelation, salvation and grace 'which reaches its goal and climax in Jesus Christ'.[40]

Nevertheless, however much living Christian faith has primacy over reflecting upon it, the Church has in fact reflected a great deal about its faith in Jesus over the centuries and articulated a highly developed body of Christological doctrine. This development took place within the New Testament itself and in the theology and Councils of the Church in subsequent ages. We look now to Rahner's contribution to this reflection in the contemporary Church.

Notes

1   FC, p. 177.

2   Ibid., p. 230.

3   'Remarks on the importance of the history of Jesus for Catholic dogmatics', TI 13, p. 212.

4   Ibid., p. 201.

5   FC, p. 238.

6   Ibid., pp. 237–8.

7   Ibid., p. 236. See, for example, John 20:31: 'What has been written here has been recorded in order that you may hold the faith that Jesus is the Christ, the Son of God, and that through this faith you may possess eternal life in his name'.

8   FC, p. 246.

9   See ibid., pp. 246–9.

10   See ibid., pp. 255–64.

11   See 'Dogmatic reflections on the knowledge and self-consciousness of Christ', TI 5, pp. 193–215.

12   FC, pp. 245–6.

13   Ibid., p. 246.

14   'Remarks on the importance of the history of Jesus for Catholic dogmatics', pp. 208–12.

15   FC, p. 240.

16   See Rahner's discussion of *Historie* and *Geschichte* in FC, pp. 240–1.

17   Ibid., p. 241.

18   Ibid., pp. 240–1.

19   Ibid., p. 230.

20   Ibid., p. 243.

21   See Luke 24:32, 35; John 20:14, 16; 21:4, 7.

22   FC, p. 266.

23   See the comments on the meaning of resurrection in Karl Rahner and Wilhelm Thüsing, *A New Christology* (London: Burns & Oates/New York: Crossroad, 1980), pp. 10–13.

24   See FC, pp. 264–82.

25   Ibid., p. 266.

26   Ibid., p. 271.

27   Ibid., pp. 268–9.

28   Ibid., p. 269.

29   Ibid., p. 276.

30   Ibid., p. 279.

31   Ibid., p. 282.

32   Ibid., pp. 283–5. See also 'The one Christ and the universality of salvation', TI 16, pp. 199–224.

33   FC, p. 195.

34   'The one Christ and the universality of salvation', p. 211.

35   FC, pp. 305–11.

36   See 'On the theology of the Incarnation', TI 4, p. 119, and *Watch and Pray with Me* (New York: Herder & Herder, 1966/London: Burns & Oates, 1968), pp. 57–8.

37 See 'Anonymous Christians', TI 6, pp. 390–8; 'Anonymous and explicit faith', TI 16, pp. 52–9.

38 GS, no. 22.

39 FC, p. 176.

40 Ibid.

5

Transcendental Christology

Applying his characteristic method of transcendental Thomism to Christological questions, Rahner develops what he calls a 'transcendental Christology'. The task of transcendental Christology is to develop an ontology and an anthropology within which the affirmation of Christian faith that Jesus is both God and man makes sense and is intelligible in our contemporary cultural situation. Theology is always a quest for meaning and understanding, and in this instance it is an effort to understand what the 'idea' of a God-Man means. This idea then becomes the *a priori* horizon within which the faith affirmation about Jesus is interpreted and understood. But Rahner hastens to clarify how this '*a priori* idea' functions:

> When we say that at least today an a priori doctrine of the God-Man must be developed in a transcendental theology, this does not mean of course that such an a priori doctrine could be developed temporally and historically prior to the actual encounter with the God-Man. We always reflect upon the conditions of possibility for a reality which we have already encountered.[1]

In one of his favourite examples, Rahner says that it is only when Beethoven has actually created his music that one realizes what the possibilities of music are. Likewise, it is only an encounter with Jesus as man and God that reveals what the God-given possibilities of human existence are. But moving from 'fact' to 'idea', and seeing the former as possible, rescues the faith affirmation that it actually happened in Jesus from the suspicion of being an unintelligible and untenable piece of mythology from an obsolete past.

In developing a transcendental Christology for today, of course, one remains tied to dogmatic statements about Jesus in Christian tradition, but sees these statements as the beginning, not the end of Christological reflection.[2] For the ideas or concepts employed in these dogmatic statements, ideas such as hypostasis, nature and hypostatic union, could have served the Church of the fourth or fifth century very well as articulations of its faith in the mystery of Jesus in that particular historical situation. But since they are ways of conceiving of this mystery, and not the mystery or the reality itself, they leave open the possibility of other ways of expressing the same faith in other historical situations. Rahner speaks, therefore, both of the 'permanent validity' and of the 'limits' of the traditional dogmatic statements about Jesus formulated at the great Councils of Nicaea (325), Ephesus (431) and Chalcedon (451).[3] Among these are the statements that he had two natures, human and divine, and that the two natures were hypostatically united in a single hypostasis or person.

Before looking at these limits it would be well to consider how Rahner understands the nature of dogmatic statements to begin with.[4] First, a dogmatic statement shares all the characteristics of human statements in general: it is related to the person or persons making it, is embedded in a historical and social fabric, uses culturally conditioned concepts and terms, contains different literary forms, and makes presuppositions shared by both speaker and listener without which communication and mutual understanding would be impossible. It is also affected by the fact that all human beings are sinners, so that a statement which is true can also be rash or presumptuous, one-sided or narrow-minded, untimely or equivocal. Moreover, since to a large extent dogmatic statements do not refer to objects of direct sense-experience, they are analogous, that is, they point to a reality beyond their representations of it, and hence there is always a tension and an unbridgeable gap between what is said and the reality that is meant and intended.[5]

Secondly, a dogmatic statement is a statement of faith in the sense that it always involves an obedient listening to God's word and the human embodiment of this word in the faith response of the listener. It always arises out of the life of faith, worship and prayer where the pre-conceptual knowledge which the statement conceptualizes and expresses is gained, and is never mere intellectual speculation or problem-solving. Hence the difference between the believer and the scientist of religion lies deeper than the mere fact that one assents to the truth of the statement and the other does not. For the scientist of religion who does not share the life of faith does not know the reality of which the proposition speaks, but only the terms of the proposition. In faith one is not just related to propositions, but also to the reality to which the propositions point.[6]

Rahner goes on to point out that dogmatic statements are ecclesiological statements, statements by the official teachers of the Church which express the common faith of the Church. Since the Church is an historical reality, it must interpret Scripture in this ongoing way in order to keep the faith alive in ever new historical situations. Such statements involve decisions about linguistic usage and rules for the language of faith. Such decisions are binding on all members of the Church, but they do not absolutize the language in the sense of identifying the language with the reality of which it speaks. For the reality itself is of incalculable richness and fullness, but all of our concepts and language are limited, and statements which bring out one aspect of the reality will inevitably leave other aspects in the background. Moreover, language is an historical reality, and terms can change their meaning.[7]

Because of these limitations of all human language, including the language of dogmatic statements, such statements do not 'contain' the truth, but point beyond themselves to an experience of the mystery itself. Finally, dogmatic statements, for all of their binding character, are not identical with the original statement of the faith in Scripture. For though Scripture, too, contains the human element of theology and is not the pure word of God, it is the word of the original witnesses, and stands as the norm which governs all subsequent articulations of the faith. Dogmatic statements acknowledge the primacy of Scripture, of which they are interpretations, not additions.[8]

In the light of these general observations about the nature of dogmatic statements, Rahner points out the limits of the Church's Christological doctrines. Granted the 'permanent validity' of the truth they express about Jesus Christ, they are by their very nature partial and not full expressions of this truth. The classical doctrine based on the notion of Incarnation is, first of all, an exclusively 'descending' Christology in the sense that it speaks *from the outset* of the incarnate Word of God who has 'come down' to us. By beginning with this ultimate mystery it jumps over the humanity of Jesus which is the point at which we have access to this ultimate mystery:

Consequently, everything is seen and understood as coming *from* above, and not as going *towards* that point. But then it really is no longer so easy to exclude mythological misunderstandings from the correct and orthodox doctrine in our consciousness and in our piety.[9]

The humanity of Jesus can be misunderstood as merely the livery which God donned in order to appear among us. The notion of Incarnation, then, should be the end and not the beginning of Christological reflection.[10]

Related to this is what Rahner calls the problem of the 'is' formulas, for example, the statement that Jesus 'is' God. This is an abiding truth of the faith if the statement is understood correctly. But we tend to understand 'is' in the same sense as in the statement 'Peter is a man', and then it is not understood correctly. For the latter statement asserts a real identification between subject and predicate, while the former asserts a unity between realities that are really different and at an infinite distance from each other. The humanity of Jesus as humanity is not God. The statement that Jesus 'is' God expresses half of the mystery, namely, that the two natures of Jesus are not separate, but it does not express the other half, that they are distinct and unmixed. Forgetting the latter and subsuming the humanity of Jesus into his divinity is the heresy of the Monophysites. Ironically, comments Rahner, this heretical understanding is often thought today to be the most radical form of the true faith.[11]

There is also a problem with the use of the term the 'person' of the Logos to designate the point wherein the two natures are united. For if the term is not understood in the sense of 'hypostasis' in the original dogmatic formula, but in its modern sense as a centre of conscious and free activity, and inevitably most people do understand it this way, there is once again the danger of the Monophysite heresy:

This would overlook the fact that the man Jesus *in* his human reality exists with a created, active and 'existentiell' centre of activity vis-à-vis God and in an absolute difference from him. He prays, he is obedient, he comes to be historically, he makes free decisions, and in a process of genuine historical development he also has new experiences which surprise him, and these are clearly in evidence in the New Testament.[12]

To forget this is to forget that Jesus was as human as we are 'in all things but sin'.

Finally, Rahner points out that neither of the terms 'hypostasis' or 'person' in the classical Christology gives clear expression to the saving significance of the hypostatic union 'for us'. This is especially true of Western Christianity which, perhaps because of Western individualism, finds the notion of the 'assumption' of the whole human race in the individual human reality of Jesus foreign to its way of thinking:

> Within this horizon of understanding, then, the hypostatic union is the constitution of a person who *performs* redemptive activity, provided that his actions are moral and that his accomplishment is accepted by God as representative for the human race. But he does not mean in his very *being* salvation, redeemer and satisfaction.[13]

It would be desirable, then, to have a formulation of the Christological doctrine which 'gave immediate expression to the *salvific* event which Jesus Christ himself *is*'.

To return to the first point, how can the classical 'descending' Christology of God becoming incarnate in the world and in humanity be supplemented by an 'ascending' Christology which begins with the world and humanity, and sees them as moving towards this point of unity with God? One way would be to understand the Christian doctrine of Incarnation within the context of an evolutionary view of the world.[14] Evolution is understood here in a general sense, as opposed to a static view of the world as made up of fixed natures or species created as such from the beginning. Should an evolutionary view provide the context for an ascending Christology, then not only is evolution as a general theory not contradictory to Christian faith, as it was thought to be and still is thought to be by some, but beyond the compatibility of the two, there would even be a positive and intrinsic affinity between them.

We can trace three main steps in Rahner's attempt to show this affinity and thereby work out an ascending Christology of the world's movement towards unity with God. First, there is the intrinsic unity of matter and spirit in the sense of the evolutionary movement of the material world towards spiritual existence.[15] Secondly, there is the intrinsic unity between human spiritual existence and the life of grace freely bestowed by God.[16] Thirdly, there is the intrinsic unity between the union of human beings with God in grace and the hypostatic union of the man Jesus with God.[17] In Rahner's cosmic vision the being of the whole created universe moves towards its fulfilment in human being, and human being moves towards its fulfilment in Jesus Christ. His cosmology, anthropology and Christology are intrinsically related moments within this single vision.

For Christian faith the unity of matter and spirit, which is a unity in difference and therefore not an identity or homogeneity, is based on the belief that all things, heaven and earth, the realm of the material and spiritual, are the creation of one and the same God. This unity of origin in a single cause means that in the midst of all the variety of created things they possess an inner similarity and commonality, that they form a single world. Matter and spirit, therefore, do not merely exist alongside each other as disparate realities, and much less are they hostile or in contradiction to each other. Christian faith has constantly had to struggle against Platonic or gnostic tendencies to see matter as the realm of evil and darkness from which spirit must seek deliverance. For it believes that the eternal Word of God 'became flesh', and it understands salvation as the 'resurrection of the flesh', and not as an escape from the realm of matter. It is to be taken for granted in Christian theology and philosophy 'that spirit and matter have more in common than they have differentiating them'.[18]

Moreover, this intrinsic relationship is not static, but has a history. It is the history of material being in its process of becoming, not just in the sense of becoming different, but becoming more:

> Becoming must be understood as becoming *more*, as the coming to be of more reality, as reaching and achieving a greater fullness of being. But this more must not be understood as simply added to what was there before. Rather it must on the one hand be the effect of what was there before, and on the other hand it must be an intrinsic increase in its own being. But this means that if becoming is really to be taken seriously it must be understood as real *self-transcendence*, as surpassing oneself, as emptiness actively achieving its own fullness.[19]

Lest in this process of active self-transcendence emptiness seem to be the source of fullness, or nothingness the ground of being, self-transcendence must be understood as taking place by the power of the absolute fullness of being. This power or dynamism must be so intrinsic to the finite being that it empowers it to achieve a real and *active* self-transcendence, but nevertheless it cannot be part of the finite being's essence or else the latter could not really become.

In the light of these reflections Rahner continues:

> Perhaps it will suffice here to propose the thesis that the notion of an active self-transcendence in which both 'self' and 'transcendence' are to be taken with equal seriousness is a logically necessary notion if the phenomenon of becoming is to be maintained. This notion of self-transcendence also includes transcendence into something substantially new, a leap to something *essentially* higher.[20]

This is possible so long as the intrinsic dynamism empowering this evolutionary process of becoming is understood as God's creative and co-operative presence as the ground of his creation. But if the world is one and is involved in a single history in which the genuinely 'new' appears, then 'there is no reason to deny that matter should have developed towards life and towards man'.[21] The lower order of reality prepares for and is a prelude to this unfolding into something higher, and the higher order includes and subsumes the lower into its new mode of existence. Since human beings are the self-transcendence of living matter in whom matter and nature become conscious of themselves, their history and the history of nature form an intrinsic, stratified unity. Hence the history of human freedom, though tied to the antecedent structures and necessities of the material world, involves not just human culture, but also an active transformation of the material world.

It is against the background of this unity that we must understand the second step of Rahner's synthesis, the intrinsic unity of nature and grace. He affirms this unity, as we have already considered (above, pp. 36–40), by conceiving of God's gracious presence in the world through his Spirit as a 'supernatural existential'. This means that in God's creative intention, from the very beginning the intrinsic dynamism and goal of the evolutionary process has been not just the transcendence of matter beyond its own power into the human life of knowledge, freedom and love, but also the transcendence of human life beyond its own power into participation in God's own life through knowledge, freedom and love. Human beings come to be so that God can share his life in this way. Hence the history of God's self-revelation in grace does not float above the history of nature and man as an added embellishment, but is imbedded within as its deepest identity.

71

From Rahner's viewpoint, then, it is impossible to conceive of the salvation of the 'soul' apart from the 'body', or to conceive of the salvation of human beings apart from their material environment and cosmos. Just as all creation is one in its origin and in the single history of its becoming, so too it is one in its goal and final consummation. Looking 'downwards', man and his material environment are of a piece, just as, looking 'upwards', man and grace are of a piece. Hence the primary Christian symbols of the end of history do not speak of the 'atomized salvation' of each individual or the beatitude of separate souls, but speak in social terms of the coming of the 'kingdom of God' and of 'a new heaven and a new earth'.[22] Against any form of Platonic dualism, all of God's creation will share in the final transformation of all things.

When the evolutionary process reaches the stage of human consciousness and freedom, history in the proper sense begins. That is, human freedom becomes a decisive factor in its course and direction. It is in the context of human freedom that Rahner in his third step sees the unique role of Jesus in this history, and the place of Christology in an evolutionary view of the world. Given that human beings are free and exist in a common history of inter-communication, it must be said of God's self-communication in grace:

> This self-communication is necessarily addressed to a free history of the human race. It can take place only in a *free* acceptance by free subjects, and indeed in a *common* history. God's self-communication does not suddenly become acosmic, directed only to an isolated and individualized subjectivity. It affects the history of the human race and is addressed to all men in their intercommunication, for it is only therein and thereby that the acceptance of God's self-communication can take place historically.[23]

This means that while the offer of God's self-communication is an existential which pervades all of history, its free acceptance is an historical event that takes place at ever definite points of time and space.

Jesus of Nazareth is seen by Christian faith as the person in whose total openness to God this offer met with a free and perfect response, so that in his life and death the history of grace reaches its irreversible and unsurpassable triumph over sin. Since the history of sin is the history of separation and alienation from God, the perfect union with God that he achieved in his free response is the undoing of sin and the entrance into history of its opposite, that is, salvation. He *is* salvation and saviour in his very being, and not just in his actions. Moreover, since his union with God is irrevocable and cannot be surpassed by a still greater union, he is the 'absolute saviour':

> We are applying this title to that historical person who appears in time and space and signifies the beginning of the absolute self-communication of God which is moving towards its goal, that beginning which indicates that this self-communication for everyone has taken place irrevocably and has been victoriously inaugurated.[24]

This does not mean that salvation begins or ends with Jesus in a temporal sense, but that in him the process that began before him and continues after him has reached its climax, not its end or conclusion. As absolute saviour Jesus must be 'both the absolute promise of God to spiritual creatures as a whole', and at the same time 'the acceptance of this self-communication' and thereby the fulfilment of the promise.[25]

In the unity of these two aspects Rahner sees the meaning of the traditional Christological term 'hypostatic union', the union of the divine and the human in a single person. Jesus is the presence of God's saving activity in the world in such a way that he is part of the world:

> He cannot simply be God himself as acting in the world, but must be a part of the cosmos, a moment within its history, and indeed at its climax. And this is also said in the Christological dogma: Jesus is truly man, truly a part of the earth, truly a moment in this world's biological process of becoming, a moment in man's natural history, for he was 'born of a woman' (Gal 4:4).[26]

Otherwise, the world would not have been truly united to God in him. At the same time, what he accepted in the fullest and most radical way was God's *self*-communication, the very life and being of God's son, so that in him God's own son became flesh:

> According to the conviction of Christian faith, Jesus is that person who, in and through what we call his obedience, his prayer

73

and his freely accepted destiny to die, also lived out the acceptance of the grace bestowed on him by God and of the immediacy
to God which he possesses as man.[27]

In this immediacy to and union with God implied in the notion of an
absolute saviour Rahner sees the same content that is expressed in
the doctrines of Incarnation and hypostatic union.

But is the hypostatic union an absolutely higher level which sur-
passes the bestowal of grace on spiritual creatures, or is it a singular
and unique moment *within* the universal history of grace? Rahner
points out that the intrinsic effect of the hypostatic union for the
humanity of Jesus is the same as the goal of all grace, namely, the
immediate vision of God which the created, human soul of Jesus
enjoys. Moreover, theology emphasizes that the Incarnation and
hypostatic union took place 'for the sake of our salvation', and do
not add any increase in reality and life to the divinity of the Logos.
They can be seen, then, as the highest and fullest instance of union
between God and man which grace by its very nature is:

> Although the hypostatic union is a unique event in its own
> essence, and viewed in itself it is the highest conceivable event, it
> is nevertheless an intrinsic moment within the whole process by
> which grace is bestowed upon all spiritual creatures.[28]

It is, then, a unique moment within the history of the world's self-
transcendence into the life of God, and seen from God's side, a
unique moment within the history of God's self-communication to
the world which makes the self-transcendence possible.

But to understand the hypostatic union within the history of grace
does not lessen or obscure its unique character. For if Jesus, in
whom God's absolute self-communication is historically present as
both offer and acceptance, is really to be the unsurpassable and
definitive offer and acceptance, then his human reality must be a
reality of God himself. If it were only a finite mediation of God, it
could in principle be surpassed. Of his human reality, then, we have
to say:

> It is not only established by God, but it is God himself. But if this
> offer is itself a human reality as graced in an absolute way, and if
> this is really and absolutely to be the offer of God himself, then
> here a human reality belongs absolutely to God, and this is

precisely what we call hypostatic union when it is understood correctly.[29]

This union is distinguished from our union with God not by what has been offered in it, namely, in both instances grace, but by the fact that Jesus is the offer for us, and we ourselves once again are not the offer, but rather the recipients of grace.

In a series of further reflections Rahner tries to show that an ascending Christology, in which the self-transcending movement of all creation towards life in God reaches its culmination in Jesus' union with God, is perfectly compatible with the traditional descending Christology which speaks of the movement of God towards the world or God becoming flesh. Indeed, they are but two sides of the same coin, or the two poles of the single union between God and the world that is the substance and heart of Christology. This descending Christology finds its classical expression in the notion of Incarnation, the idea that the 'Word became flesh' (John 1:14). Taking each element individually, Rahner asks what we mean when we say that the Word of God became man.[30]

Beginning with the element which seems to be the most intelligible part of the assertion, what do we mean by the term 'man'? Here is something that we know about both from the inside in our own personal experiences, and from the outside in other persons, and in all the arts and sciences which deal with the human. We can to some extent distinguish between the basic structure of the human and its accidental modifications, and speak of 'human nature'. The faith assertion that God became man would mean, then, that God assumed an individual human nature. But can we really define what human nature is?

If by 'definition' we mean a delimiting formula which enumerates all the elements of which a reality is composed, each element itself being able to be defined, a definition of human nature is impossible. Even the classical definition of man as a 'rational animal' leaves open the question what 'rational' means. For we can say what man is only if we say what he has to do with and what concerns him. But in his rational nature man is quite literally boundless, open to an unlimited horizon which is nameless and indefinable. In our transcendence we confront what is incomprehensible and unfathomable, the absolute mystery we call God. Although, then, we can learn much about human reality and to some extent define partial aspects of it, man in his totality and by his very nature is a mystery to himself.

This clarifies what it means to say that God assumes a human nature as his own:

> If this indefinable nature, whose limit, that is, its 'definition', is this unlimited orientation towards the infinite mystery of fullness, is assumed by God *as his own* reality, then it has reached the very point towards which it is always moving by virtue of its essence. It is its very *meaning* ... to be given away and to be handed over, to be that being who realizes himself and finds himself by losing himself once and for all in the incomprehensible.[31]

This happens in the strictest and most radical sense when a human nature so empties and gives itself to the mystery of God that it becomes God's own human nature. Seen from this perspective, God's incarnation or assumption of a human nature is the unique and fullest actualization of the very essence of human reality. Nor is this merely a 'consciousness Christology'. Rather it transposes the traditional ontic understanding of human nature into an ontological understanding in which human, spiritual nature is understood analogically, not univocally, with non-spiritual natures.

Rahner then moves to the second term of the faith affirmation and asks 'Can God really *become* something?' This presents a special difficulty, for it is the traditional teaching of both Christian philosophy and theology that God cannot become, that God is the fullness of being and pure act, and therefore is immutable and changeless. The apparent dilemma is resolved in the tradition by declaring that 'the becoming and the change are on the side of the created reality which is assumed', but they do not touch the eternal, immutable Logos:

> Hence all becoming and all history and the laborious effort connected with them still remain on this side of the absolute abyss which separates the immutable, necessary God from the mutable, conditional and historical world in its process of becoming, and which admits of no admixture between them.[32]

But it still remains true that the Logos *became* man, and therefore 'the history of the becoming of this human reality became *his own* history' and his own reality. How, then, can the assertion of God's immutability not make us lose sight of the other truth?:

> What took place in Jesus as becoming and as history here in our midst, in our space, in our time and world, in our process of

becoming, in our evolution and in our history, that this is precisely the history of the Word of God himself, *his own* becoming.[33]

Fidelity to the fundamental dogma of the Incarnation forces us, then, to say that in some sense God can indeed become something.

Rahner formulates this sense by saying that God 'who is not subject to change in himself can *himself* be subject to change *in something else*', in some other which he freely chooses to make his own.[34] He does not intend this formulation to offer a positive insight into the compatibility of immutability and becoming in God, but rather to see the two truths in a dialectical relationship: each must be understood as not denying the other, nor is either truth subordinate to the other. The relationship is parallel to the dialectic which says that the divine and human natures of Jesus are *both* unmixed *and* inseparate. They are unmixed and distinct, so that the becoming is on the side of the human, but they are also inseparate, so that it is the Logos *himself* who becomes in his human nature. It is the same kind of dialectic as when we must understand that God is one in such a way that we do not deny that God is also three, and vice versa.

Nor is this kind of becoming in God a sign of need or deficiency; it is rather the height of his perfection. God can not only create what is different from himself, but 'He possesses the possibility of *establishing* the other as his own reality by dispossessing *himself*, by giving *himself* away' in an act of kenosis or self-emptying.[35] Moreover, the Logos did not assume an already existing human nature, but his self-emptying *is* the creation and the assumption of the human nature as his own reality: he 'creates by assuming' and 'assumes by creating'. From this perspective God's capacity to create without giving himself is a secondary and derivative possibility grounded in this fuller possibility of creating in order to share himself. Creatures must be understood, then, as created by God in their own reality with the deeper possibility, the *potentia oboedientialis*, to be 'the *grammar of God's possible self-expression*'.[36]

In the light of this, Rahner arrives at a deeper understanding of the third element in the faith affirmation: *the Logos* became flesh, indeed, that it could only be the Logos. For the Logos as the self-expression of the Father in the inner-trinitarian life of God is the condition which makes possible the self-expression of God outwards, and the latter is the identical expression of the former:

If this God expresses his very own self into the *emptiness* of what is not God, then this expression is the outward expression of his immanent Word, and not something arbitrary which could also be proper to another divine person.[37]

There are human beings who are not the Logos, and there could be human beings even if the Logos had not become man. Otherwise the Incarnation would not be due to God's sovereign freedom. There can be the lesser without the greater, but the possibility of the lesser is grounded in the more radical possibility of a creature being the expression of God's own Word.

Moreover, the humanity of the Word does not exist antecedently, but is that which comes to be in the utterance and is the utterance. Jesus as man and precisely in his humanity *is* the Word of God. Otherwise the humanity of the Logos would not reveal God but disguise him, except perhaps revealing him by speaking about him. But then the Incarnation would be superfluous for the same words could have been delivered through a prophet:

> The man Jesus must be the self-revelation of God through who he is and not only through his words, and this he really cannot be if precisely this humanity were not the expression of God.[38]

From this perspective humanity can be understood 'as that which comes to be when God's self-expression, his Word, is uttered into the emptiness of the Godless void in love', or by saying that 'when God wants to be what is not God, man comes to be'.[39] This is to understand humanity in terms of its highest and uniquely graced instance, the man Jesus, and does not deny the difference between him and the lesser instance of God's self-communication in grace to all humanity.

To conceive of the humanity of Jesus itself as the self-expression of God is to conceive of it as the 'real symbol' of God.[40] A real symbol is one in which the reality of what is symbolized is really present in the symbol and therefore can come to expression in the symbol. Unlike a sign which is only extrinsically or arbitrarily related to the signified to which it points, a real symbol has an intrinsic, ontological relationship to what is symbolized so that it makes it present. Such a relationship is possible because being is symbolic: 'all beings are by their nature symbolic because they necessarily "express" themselves in order to attain their own nature'.[41] The human soul as the form of the body, for instance, comes to expression in the body as its symbol, and has no existence apart from its expression in symbol: the symbol 'is the self-realization of a being in the other which is constitutive of its essence'.[42] Body and soul are really one, but in the differentiated unity of symbol and symbolized.

Rahner sees the supreme instance of the symbolic nature of reality in the inner-trinitarian life of God himself.[43] God's being is such that the Father expresses himself in the Word and is himself as Father in this expression. Likewise, the Word exists in and through being the expression, the symbol of the Father. They are of the same essence and they are one in the differentiated unity of symbol and symbolized. If in his sovereign freedom God speaks his Word outwards, that which comes to be is his created expression in space and time, his eternal Word become flesh. The humanity of Jesus, then, is the real symbol in which the reality of God becomes present and finds expression. His humanity and divinity vary not in indirect but in direct proportion; the more truly human he is, the more fully is he God's own son.

In the light of Rahner's evolutionary view of Christology, this process wherein the Word becomes flesh is identical with the process wherein flesh becomes the Word of God. Descending and ascending Christology, God's self-communication and man's acceptance, the Incarnation of God and the divinization of man are in each instance two sides of the same coin. Hence the Incarnation is not an abrupt interruption or aberration in the 'normal' course of history, but the 'fullness of time', the culmination of a movement which began with creation itself. This 'idea' of the God-Man is a more universal and more intrinsic way of understanding and expressing for our age what Christian faith affirms of Jesus of Nazareth. It is an attempt to avoid other 'ideas': mythological ones which see God in human disguise, or monophysite ones that find Christ by going around the humanity of Jesus, or gnostic ones whose route to God lies outside the world and human history altogether. It is not the case, says Rahner, that God is in heaven and we are on earth. Rather, 'we have to say of the God whom we profess in Christ that he is exactly where we are, and only there is he to be found'.[44] Theology is also and always anthropology, and Christology is the beginning and end of anthropology.

But if Jesus was the culmination of a history that began before him, he is also the beginning of a history that continues on after him. This is the history of the Church, the community of those who believed in him and continued to proclaim him and his message to the world.

Notes

1 FC, p. 177.

2 See the reflections on the Council of Chalcedon as both end and beginning in 'Current problems in Christology', TI 1, pp. 149–200.

3 Ibid., pp. 285–93.

4 See 'What is a dogmatic statement?', TI 5, pp. 42–66.

5 Ibid., pp. 44–7.

6 Ibid., pp. 48–51.

7 Ibid., pp. 51–8.

8 Ibid., pp. 58–66.

9 FC, pp. 289–90.

10 Ibid., p. 177.

11 Ibid., pp. 290–1.

12 Ibid., p. 292.

13 Ibid., pp. 292–3.

14 See 'Christology within an evolutionary view of the world', TI 5, pp. 157–92, and FC, pp. 178–203.

15 See 'The unity of spirit and matter in the Christian understanding of faith', TI 6, pp. 153–77.

16 See 'Nature and grace', TI 4, pp. 165–88.

17 See 'Christology within an evolutionary view of the world', pp. 173–92.

18 FC, p. 182.

19 Ibid., p. 184.

20 Ibid., p. 185.

21 Ibid., pp. 185–6.

22 See 'The unity of spirit and matter in the Christian understanding of faith', p. 162. TI 6.

23 FC, p. 193.

24 Ibid., pp. 193–4.

25 Ibid., p. 195.

26 Ibid.

27 Ibid.

28 Ibid., p. 201.

29 Ibid., p. 202.

30   See 'On the theology of the Incarnation', TI 4, pp. 105–20, and FC, pp. 212–28.

31   FC, p. 217.

32   Ibid., p. 220.

33   Ibid.

34   Ibid.

35   Ibid., p. 222.

36   Ibid., pp. 222–3.

37   Ibid., p. 223.

38   Ibid., p. 224.

39   Ibid., pp. 224–5.

40   See 'The theology of the symbol', TI 4, pp. 221–52.

41   Ibid., p. 224.

42   Ibid., p. 234.

43   Ibid., pp. 235–40.

44   FC, p. 226.

6

The Church

Approaching the Church as a systematic theologian, Rahner draws on the same principles that he employed to understand grace, and, more specifically, Jesus Christ as the supreme moment of grace. The history of God's offer of grace is universal, but the acceptance in faith which makes it incarnate and present in the world is always a particular event. The event of Jesus' life, death and resurrection is the irreversible triumph of grace in him, and the irrevocable promise of its triumph for the world. The Church is the community of faith which believes in this triumph in him, that is, believes in his cross and resurrection, and it is the community of hope which trusts in the promise of its final triumph for the world, called his second coming or the coming of God's kingdom. Hence the 'already' character of its kerygma, 'God raised him to life again' (Acts 2:24), or 'He was raised to life on the third day' (1 Cor 15:4), and the 'not yet' character of its prayer, 'Come, Lord Jesus!' (Rev 22:20), or 'Thy kingdom come' (Matt 6:10). Rahner understands the Church as the community which must keep this faith and hope alive 'until he comes'.

He often pointed to a text of the Second Vatican Council which throws light on the nature of this task. Speaking of Tradition, the Council says:

And so the Church, in her teaching, life and worship, perpetuates and hands on to all generations all that she herself is, all that she believes.[1]

The text speaks of Tradition first as the Church handing on what she *is*, and secondly as handing on what she *believes*. The faith and hope of the Church are fundamentally a way of being and a way of life, a praxis, and in a secondary, although necessary, sense theoretical statements of belief and hope. To the extent that the community is living this faith and hope, which is the faith and hope of Jesus himself, it is living by his Spirit and is the ongoing embodiment of his Spirit. Paul says to the community at Corinth which has received his Spirit, 'You are the body of Christ' (1 Cor 12:27),[2] and to express this unity John uses the image of branches drawing sap and life from the vine (John 15:5). In accordance with these biblical images Rahner understands the Church as the sacrament or real symbol of Christ.[3]

Before looking at his explanation of this, it would be well to note the various realities that are referred to by the single term 'Church'. Although in recent centuries the term has come to be understood by Catholics as referring to the worldwide institutional Church, one of the accomplishments of the Second Vatican Council was to have recovered other and equally important senses.[4] Among these is Church in the sense of the local community or parish which gathers in worship to hear the word of God and celebrate the Eucharist. Rahner quotes the Council:

> The Church of Christ is truly present (*vere adest*) in all lawfully instituted local communities of the faithful who, united with their pastors, are actually called 'Churches' in the New Testament itself ... In these communities, however poor and small they may be, and even though they may live in the diaspora, Christ is present, Christ through whose power the one holy Catholic and apostolic Church is united.[5]

In the New Testament usage referred to, the local community was not *a* Church, but *the* Church, that is, 'the whole is truly present and achieves its fullness in the part'.[6] The local community is not merely an administrative subdivision of a larger organization called Church, but is the concrete reality of what Church is: the presence of Christ and his Spirit. This is the deepest truth that can be asserted of the Universal Church, and it is also true of every community gathered around the Eucharist.

Rahner explains why the Council wanted to include this understanding of Church in its teaching:

There was a desire to see the Church as she exists in the concrete in everyday life, as present where she actually celebrates the death of the Lord, breaks the bread of the word of God, prays, loves and bears the cross of human existence, where she acquires a reality that is truly palpable ... and is something more than an abstract ideology or a dogmatic thesis ...[7]

It is here that one has the most basic and most direct religious experience of Church and discovers its theological meaning. It is here where the presence of Christ is made real in the preaching of the Gospel and the celebration of the Eucharist that the Church can have an impact. The local community, of course, will be conscious of being united with all the other communities which are also this same Church, and see its identity within this larger whole. But all further understanding of the Church must draw its life from this Eucharistic centre.[8]

Taking into account, then, these different levels on which the Church exists, and by analogy with his use of the term 'real symbol' to express the relationship of Jesus to God, Rahner says of the Church:

Now the Church is the continuance, the contemporary presence, of that real, eschatologically triumphant and irrevocably established presence in the world, in Christ, of God's salvific will. The Church is the abiding presence of that primal sacramental word of definitive grace, which Christ is in the world, effecting what is uttered by uttering it in sign. By the very fact of being in that way the enduring presence of Christ in the world, the Church is truly the fundamental sacrament, the well-spring of the sacraments in the strict sense.[9]

The Church in the sense of the community of believers is the sacrament or real symbol of union with God through Christ and in his Spirit, first of all, for its own members who have been incorporated into the community through baptism. Prior to this incorporation, every human being is already a child of God and a brother or sister of Jesus Christ by virtue of the universal call to grace and the 'consecration' of all humanity through the Incarnation:

In as far as mankind, thus 'consecrated', is a real unity from the very start, there already exists a *'people of God'* which extends as far as humanity itself, even before any social and juridical organization of mankind as a supernatural unity in a Church.[10]

The Christian community brings this prior reality to concrete, historical expression and makes it a visible, tangible, social and public reality. Entrance into the Church is a new and fuller way of being what one already is.

But given the social nature of human existence as an existence in relationship to other persons, all of whom together are called to be God's people, this new way is also a necessary way. Christianity cannot be just an amorphous collection of believing individuals, but must be a believing community, a Church.[11] The tradition has always taught that the Church is a necessary means of salvation, indeed, that 'outside the Church there is no salvation'. This does not mean for Rahner that the Church is merely the 'dispenser of these means of grace for the individual's salvation', or 'the supplier of heavenly treasures' for each individual.[12] Rather the Church is the community wherein the social dimension of grace becomes visible. It is the communion of persons which mediates communion with God.

An understanding of the community's role in mediating grace to the individual can be clarified by reflection on its opposite, the mediation of evil and sin. Grace has a social dimension just as evil and sin have a social dimension. The freedom of each individual to choose good or evil exists in a context and milieu that is shaped and determined by the goodness or the guilt of others. Since this is true of every individual and has been so from the beginning, the tradition speaks of 'original sin',[13] the sin that has affected the human race going all the way back to its origin. But grace, too, can have such social affects, as Paul brings out in the contrast he draws between Adam and Christ, between the origin of sin and the origin of grace (Rom 5:12-17). The community that is the real symbol of Christ and the embodiment of his grace is the social milieu wherein grace can be encountered and become effective. In this sense the Church is the 'fundamental sacrament' and effective sign of grace for its members.

But there is a second and equally important sense in which Rahner views the reality of the Church as sacramental. It is a sacrament not only of the salvation of its members, but also 'the basic sacrament of the salvation of the world'. This means that:

The Church is the concrete historical *manifestation*, in the dimension of a history that has acquired an eschatological significance, and in the social dimension, of precisely *that* salvation which is achieved through the grace of God throughout the entire length and breadth of humanity.[14]

Because the entire human family already exists as the people of God prior to the Church, and is constituted as such by God's universal saving will which became final and definitive in the history of Jesus, the community which bears the name of Jesus manifests what is true of all people. One of the contexts in which Rahner approaches this question is the apparent contradiction between affirming the necessity of the Church for salvation, and at the same time affirming the possibility of salvation outside the Church.[15] How can both affirmations be true?

They can be reconciled only if the reality of the Church is understood as in some sense 'stratified':

The stratification referred to here is to be understood in the sense that the Church, as something visible and as sign of the union with God by grace, must itself be composed of a further twofold reality, viz. Church as an established juridical organization in the sacred order, and 'Church as humanity consecrated by the Incarnation'.[16]

Rahner refers to Church in this broader sense as 'the people of God', and sees the Church in the usual sense as the historical manifestation, the sacrament of the former. Membership in the Church through baptism, therefore, is sacrament and expression of one's belonging to God's people.

But all of God's people who are not members of the Church have, nevertheless, an intrinsic relationship to the Church because they are related to Christ. Since their relationship is not expressed but remains nameless, Rahner calls them implicit or 'anonymous Christians'.[17] He applies this term to members of non-Christian religions,[18] and maintains that these religions themselves are not simply false, but can be the social and historical mediation of grace.[19] He also applies it to people who consider themselves atheists but live in fidelity to their conscience, for grace can be mediated by realities which are not explicitly religious.[20]

Seen in the social context of the Church and of the broader reality of the people of God, it is clear that the 'supernatural existential' affects not just individuals, but has social implications as well. It is the Spirit of God present in all of human history calling and forming humankind into the unity of a single human family and a single people of God. As the counter-force in human history to original sin, it is 'original grace', indeed, the more original and deeper of the two. The Church is called to be the sacrament of this grace and the embodiment of this unity, but it is sacrament only in an imperfect and analogous sense. For the Church is also 'the Church of sinners'.[21]

The sinfulness of the Church is significant for Rahner not because it is an all too obvious fact of everyday experience, but because it is part of the Church's faith. If it were not, then our experience of the sinful Church could lead one to turn from the actual, concrete, historical Church and look for what the creed professes to be the 'holy' Church elsewhere, perhaps in a pure and spiritual communion of one's own choosing. One might find one's ideal there, but would not find God. For our faith professes that the true Church, while holy, also includes sinful members, and if this is so, then we must also say that *'the Church is sinful'*.[22] For if we were to think that sinful members have nothing to do with the 'real' Church, our real Church would actually be a disembodied idea or ideal, not the Church as it actually exists:

> But if she is something real, and if her members are sinners and as sinners remain members, then she herself is sinful. Then the sins of her children are a blot and a blemish on the holy mystical Body of Christ itself. The Church is a sinful Church: this is a truth of faith, not an elementary fact of experience. And it is a shattering truth.[23]

Rahner sees this as an important but forgotten truth in our understanding of the Church.

For it is true not just of 'ordinary' members of the Church, but of officials and administrators as well, and can 'influence very substantially their concrete mode of action as official representatives of the Church'.[24] For when the Church teaches and proclaims its message, or when it makes decisions or fails to make them when they should be made, these actions are carried out not by an abstract principle or by the Holy Spirit alone, but by the concrete men who hold office in the Church. No doctrine of the Church maintains that the Holy Spirit is a guarantee against such sinful influence. Hence 'the Church can be sinful in her actions', and 'can distort by her sin the eternal visible presence of Christ in the world which she is'.[25] Awareness that the Church is not only holy but also sinful prevents any 'arrogance' or false 'superiority' in the Church's attitude towards the world or non-Christian religions as she strives to be the sacrament of universal salvation.

It is through the presence of the Spirit given to all of its members through baptism that the Church, both local and universal, can fulfil this mission. But the one Spirit is present in a variety of gifts or 'charisms' (1 Cor 12:4), giving different members different tasks and roles in the one 'body of Christ'. In the most general differentiation of charisms, Rahner distinguishes between the charisms which accompany office and official ministry in the Church, and 'non-institutional charisms':

> It would be just as false, however, if one were to suppose that the charismatic element in the Church is reserved to her official ministry. There are, in fact, earnest Catholics who are anxious to have a right mind about the Church and hold the view, tacitly and in the background, but all the more operative and dangerous on that account, that the hierarchy is the only vehicle of the Spirit or the only portal through which the Spirit enters the Church. They imagine the Church as a sort of centralized state, and a totalitarian one at that.[26]

There is a sense in which the Church is 'absolute' for a Catholic in that it is the indefectible presence of God's grace and truth in the world. But since its authority is 'valid within certain limits and strictly circumscribed', it is not absolute in a totalitarian sense.[27] Rather the Church has a 'dual structure', possessing not only hierarchical or 'monarchical' elements, but also 'democratic' elements in the sense that the power of the Spirit is not centred in a single authority, but operates both within official channels and outside them.[28] Freedom and authority are equally essential elements of the community's life.

Rahner has written extensively on both poles of the Church's 'divinely willed' bipolar structure, including the fact that it is willed by God or is *de iure divino*. In what sense can it be said that the Church as we know it was founded by Jesus Christ who intended it to have a hierarchical structure of Pope and bishops and an infallible teaching authority? Rahner begins with a 'common conviction' of Christian Churches:

Jesus 'founded' his church. This is the common conviction of the Christian churches as long as we prescind from the question what 'founding' means ... Wherever ecclesial Christianity is found, it is convinced that it has its origins in Christ.[29]

The traditional interpretation, namely, that the historical Jesus explicitly founded the Church along with many elements in its hierarchical structure, has become very problematic today. The first among these problems is that Jesus proclaimed the kingdom of God and seemed to have expected the imminent coming of this final kingdom, in which case the founding of a Church would not have been his intention or concern. Secondly, the Churches of the New Testament period seem to have been organized in a variety of ways, and do not present a highly structured and uniform picture in accordance with some presumed intention of Jesus. How is 'founding' to be interpreted in the light of this historical evidence?[30]

Although it must be granted that Jesus did gather a group of disciples around him during his earthly life and that Peter was given a privileged position among them, Rahner prefers to interpret 'founding' in the sense of the 'provenance' or origin of the Church in Jesus,[31] and more precisely in his death and resurrection:

The Church comes from the death and resurrection of Jesus as an aspect of the lasting eschatological value of the crucified and risen Christ.[32]

There must be a Church in the sense of a community of those who believe in the crucified and risen Christ as the definitive victory of God's grace. It is only in this way that this grace and its promise can be permanently and historically present in the world until the end of time. Such a community needs some form of social organization, but does its origin in Christ imply anything about how it is to be structured and organized?

It seems clear that at the beginning the different communities of faith had various forms of social organization, and that Peter, for example, played practically no role in the Pauline communities. Nevertheless, among the various options that were available to it in the course of its historical development, the Church did make certain decisions about how it was to be organized and structured. So long as these decisions were in accordance with the nature of the

Church, although not necessarily required by that nature, and at least if these decisions were taken during the apostolic period of the Church, they can be binding and irreversible decisions for all later generations of the Church.[33] Rahner sees the emerging hierarchical structure of the papacy and episcopacy as included in such decisions. In this historical sense they can be said to be willed by God or to be *de iure divino*.[34]

But the history of the Church, of course, is still unfolding, and therefore fidelity to the past does not preclude the possibility of change in the present and future. Rahner saw the Second Vatican Council as an important moment in the modern history of the Church, and devoted much attention to questions about the hierarchical structure of the Church which the Council addressed. One such question about which there were and are different opinions concerns the relationship between the authority of the Pope and the college of bishops. Rahner's approach is to stress the collegial principle in Church governance, namely, that authority accrues to the Pope precisely as the head of the college of bishops:

> The bearer of the highest and supreme power in the Church is the united episcopate with and under the pope as its head ... Thus there is only one subject endowed with supreme power in the Church: the college of bishops assembled under the pope as its head. But there are two modes in which this supreme college may act: a 'collegiate act' properly so-called, and the act of the pope as head of the college.[35]

Rahner insists that the papal office does not stand over against or above the college of bishops or the Church as a whole. Rather the Pope is a member of the Church and a member of the college and derives his authority from his unique role *within* these bodies. One practical consequence of this would be a more active collaboration of the bishops with the Pope in the governance of the Universal Church.[36]

Rahner stresses the same collegial principle when he discusses the exercise of the episcopal office itself. Indeed, he thinks it conceivable and in accordance with Church doctrine that the episcopal office itself could be exercised by a collegiate body rather than by a single individual:

> As I see it, we could in principle and as a matter of abstract speculation even go a step further and put the hypothesis that it

would not be unequivocally contrary to the Catholic doctrine of the episcopal office to say that this episcopal authority could be borne by a *collegium*.[37]

In fact, however, in the Church's teaching on the episcopal office it is tacitly assumed that the office is borne by a single individual as has been the case historically. But there is no explicit teaching that this must necessarily be the case.

The Church has broad scope in 'creatively reshaping' this and other offices to make them more effective in the present. For office and official ministry in the Church are ultimately one, and the Church can break them down into specific offices of various kinds and degrees according to the demands of the time. Just as in 1970 the International Commission of Theologians unanimously recommended that the Pope devise rules for the way in which he might collaborate with the college of bishops rather than leaving this up to *ad hoc* decisions, so too the local bishop could do the same for those bodies which share in the direction of the local Church.[38]

Among the powers vested in the Pope and the bishops as the Church's official *magisterium* is the power to teach in an authoritative and binding way.[39] Rahner calls for closer co-operation and dialogue between bishops and theologians, comparing them to the bones and muscles in a body, each having its own nature and function, yet each needing the other to function properly.[40] On the controversial issue of the meaning and scope of infallible teaching he maintains that it applies to the '*individual* defined proposition as such', and not merely to the abiding union of the Church with Christ as a single whole, in which case 'even in "definitions" errors in individual cases can occur' and exist for a time.[41] In denying the latter, however, he does not mean that giving absolute assent to an infallible proposition excludes all criticism, for even defined dogmas are open to further historical development.

Moreover, in Rahner's opinion, 'In the foreseeable future there will be no further really new definitions'.[42] He points to the fact that the Second Vatican Council attempted no new definitions, and to the situation of pluralism in philosophy, theology and culture in which the Church exists. Such a situation argues against the likelihood of being able to formulate new propositions that will express the conscious faith of the whole Church.

The Second Vatican Council also gave some attention to two

other offices that developed in the early Church besides the office of bishop. They are the offices of priest and deacon, and Rahner reflects on the theological importance of each. He sees the 'fundamental point' of the Council's decision to restore the permanent diaconate not in a 'romantic revival' of the past, but in the recognition through sacramental ordination of tasks which are in fact already being performed in the Church, including social and charitable works for the poor. Such recognition is an acknowledgement of their necessity and importance in the Church of the present.[43]

Questions have been raised about the social role of the priest today in a Church in which the laity have become more educated and in a society which has become more secular.[44] Rahner sees the starting point in the New Testament for seeking a basis for the role of the priest not in the power to celebrate the Eucharist, since it is not clear in the New Testament that a special 'power' to celebrate the Eucharist was recognized, but in the role of leadership in a Christian community.[45] In view of the variety of tasks, functions and ministries which priests have in fact performed in the course of Church history, there is much room today for structuring the priesthood in a way that meets the needs of the contemporary Church. This includes the relationship between priests and bishop in the leadership of a particular local Church, which could be less monarchical and more collegial in structure.[46] On the controversial issue of the ordination of women, Rahner thinks that the fundamental question whether the lack of women priests is due to a 'divine tradition', or to a human tradition based on social and cultural reasons, has not been definitively settled. There is need, then, for further study and discussion in the Church.[47]

Finally, Rahner has reflected on two other institutional aspects of the Church which are in line with the 'collegial' or 'decentralizing' thread running through the teaching of Vatican II. One concerns the growing importance of bishops' conferences in the contemporary Church. Since every bishop is a member of the episcopal college, the successor to the apostolic college, every bishop has certain functions and responsibilities with regard to the Universal Church, and not just in his own diocese. This is the doctrinal basis for the existence and authority of a bishops' conference.[48] Following the principle of subsidiarity, the enormous cultural differences among the national and regional Churches within the Universal Church, and the different pastoral problems and challenges facing them, would recommend a more active role for bishops' conferences in the governance of these Churches.[49]

Secondly, the increasing frequency of pastoral synods in local Churches presents an opportunity for shared decision-making by clergy and laity in these Churches. Such democratic participation in Church governance is certainly doctrinally legitimate, but some doubt that it is desirable. If this doubt is based on the fear that the Church would be led astray by such democratic processes, one should remember that 'God's grace can ultimately speaking just as well preserve the people of God in the truth of the Gospel as popes or bishops'.[50] It was on the occasion of such a pastoral synod in Germany that Rahner made some very practical suggestions for structural changes in the German Church.

He points out that the growing secularzation of society and the declining membership of the Church have produced a radically changed situation for the Church in Germany. It has moved from being a *Volkskirche* or an accepted part of national life to being a 'diaspora' Church, a 'small flock' faced with either hostility or indifference by secular society.[51] Such a radical change calls for a radically new shape of the Church. It must show that its teaching is rooted in the Gospel, and not expect that it will be accepted merely on Church authority which is no longer taken for granted. It must have the courage to make concrete directives for action and not merely repeat general principles, and must do its moral teaching without moralizing. It must be a declericalized and open Church, one concerned not about itself but with service to others.[52] Finally, it must include 'base communities' which are formed 'from below' by the free decision of their members.[53]

Rahner bases these and many other suggestions on his general principle for the possibility of change in the Church. We tend to think that some things can change and some cannot. But everything which can be said to be unchangeable in the Church because 'divinely ordained' has come to exist in some particular historical form which we cannot identify which the unchangeable itself. For in the Church:

> The changeable and the unchangeable are not two entities simply existing side by side as immediately empirically apprehensible each in its own right.[54]

Rather it is precisely *in* the changeable, historical form that what is the unchangeable exists. At times the Church must discover new forms in which it can maintain its unchanging identity and accomplish its mission in new historical situations.

One consequence of Rahner's theological reflections on the institutional or hierarchical aspects of the Church is to restore to its rightful place in our understanding of the Church the second and equally important pole of the Church's dual structure. He calls this latter pole variously the 'dynamic' or the 'charismatic' or the 'prophetic' element in the Church. All these terms point to the fact that it is the Spirit given to all the members of the Church that is the source of the Church's life, and the stirrings of this life cannot be institutionalized or contained completely within certain structures or channels. The Second Vatican Council moved towards this broader understanding of the Church. It explicitly referred to the charismatic element, and in its Constitution on the Church it placed the second chapter concerning the people of God before the third chapter concerning Church officials. But in spite of this it must be admitted that the official Church 'still continues constantly to occupy the centre of the ecclesiological stage' in Catholic thinking.[55]

This imbalance calls for redress on both theological and sociological grounds. First, from a theological point of view:

When we consider that the distinctive characteristic of the Church, as compared with the Old Testament synagogue, consists precisely in the fact that she constitutes the presence of grace as irreversibly victorious, and that the difference between these two is not to be found in their institutional aspects as such, then it should in reality be perfectly possible to regard the Church primarily as the historical concretization of the charismatic as brought about by the Spirit of Christ, and to regard the specifically institutional element in her simply as one of the regulating factors (albeit a necessary one) for this charismatic element.[56]

The Church which must bear witness to the presence of this grace in the world consists of all the people of God, not just its officials, and every member of the Body of Christ 'has a quite specific function to perform in that Body'.[57]

Hence while Church membership requires living within certain structures, and being subject to the common rules and regulations that are necessary in any organization and institution for the well-being of the whole, every member of the Church remains at the same time a unique, free and responsible individual.[58] The term 'charism', moreover, must not necessarily be understood to mean something extraordinary or unusual. There are such gifts in the Church, but grace also manifests itself in 'hidden fidelity', 'unselfish kindness' and an 'uncompromising profession of truth', in the life of patient nurse or selfless mother, and wherever faith, hope and love are being lived, whether in 'heartfelt joy' or in the 'patience of the cross'.[59]

Approaching the same question from a sociological point of view, Rahner states the following thesis:

> The charismatic element in the Church designates that point in the Church at which God as Lord of the Church presides over the Church as an open system.[60]

An open system is one which is defined and directed not by a point immanent within the system itself, but one outside, which in the case of the Church is the Lordship of God. This means that the juridical dimension is only one element in the social reality of the Church, and one that cannot dominate over the total reality and functioning of the other elements even at the social level. Rahner sees implications of this in the legal sphere, for example, in the doctrine that a new law needs to be accepted by the people of the Church. It also has implications for the process of discovering or preserving the truth of the Church's faith, where the official *magisterium* is only one element in this process.[61] That the Church is an open system in this sense means ultimately that the charismatic is not one element in the system, but is 'transcendental in character', a characteristic of the system as a whole.

In such a system there will inevitably be tensions and conflicts between institution and charism, between authority and freedom, which raise the question of obedience in the Church. From what has been said it is clear that obedience is one virtue in the Church, but not the only one nor the one in which all else is subsumed.[62] Nor are there theoretical principles that can resolve all conflicts between Church authority and individual conscience. A practical rule of thumb might say that authority has the last word, but taking the future into account there is no last word in the proper sense. Hence the legitimate institutional element in the Church is always 'encompassed by the charismatic movement of the Spirit' which is the primary element and 'constitutes the true pith and essence of the Church'.[63] For Rahner, then, the need for dialogue between bishops and theologians,[64] and the need for 'free speech', 'public opinion'[65] and channels of communication among all segments of the Church is not just a concession to modern sensibilities, but essential to the life and mission of the Church.

During the many years of his reflections on the nature of the Church Rahner was also involved in ecumenical discussions with representatives of other Christian denominations. He was acutely aware that disunity among Christians was a counter-sign to what the Christian Church should be, and that reunion of the various traditions that have developed would be mutually enriching.[66] In his later years, while valuing the accomplishments of ecumenical discussions of past controversies, he came to question whether this was a fruitful direction for the future. He recommended a new approach which he summed up in two theses.

First, we must recognize and value the unity among the Churches that is already present on the preconceptual level of faith.

> In the Spirit of God all of us 'know' something more simple, more true and more real than we can know or express at the level of our theological concepts.[67]

We are trying to move, then, not from sheer division to unity, but from one kind of unity to another. In his second thesis he suggests that ecumenical theology turn from the past to the future. If each Church tries to develop a theology which can present the Christian message to the world of today and tomorrow, the various theologies themselves will be moving closer together.[68]

Rahner points out that all the Churches have a new and common 'partner', the secularized world in which we are living, and in learning how to talk to this partner they will be learning how to talk with one another. A post-Christian world in the sense of a world in which Christian faith is not a decisive force in society calls for a post-Christian theology, likewise in this sense.[69] Moreover, we should pay more attention to the 'non-theological' aspects of ecumenical theology, for example, secular influences on the various theologies from the history of ideas, from their 'social relevance' in various societies, and from the various languages in which they have been expressed. Doing ecumenical theology in this 'indirect' way can produce a deeper understanding of differences and the possibility of overcoming them.

It must also be admitted that most members of the various Christian denominations do not have any real knowledge of the theological differences dividing them. There are different Christians because they have grown up in different Churches; the Churches do not exist because of these different Christians. Would it not be possible to move towards an institutional unity that would recognize this wide-ranging unity of faith as well as the doctrinal differences?

Together with his colleague Heinrich Fries, Rahner tried to respond to this question in a bold and imaginative way. Convinced that the ecumenical movement had reached something of an impasse, but equally convinced that 'The unity of the Church is the commandment of the Lord of the Church', they collaborated on a joint proposal outlining how Church unity is an actual possibility today.[70] Their proposal takes the form of eight theses, each one accompanied by a lengthy commentary explaining and justifying it. The basis of this unity is their common heritage, the fundamental truths of Holy Scripture, the Apostles' Creed and the Councils of Nicaea and Constantinople accepted as binding on all partner Churches. Beyond this no partner Church can reject as incompatible with the faith what is binding dogma in another Church, but neither is this latter imposed on any other Church.

For the sake of unity this mutual 'tolerance' and 'suspension of judgement' is justified for the time being until a broader consensus is reached in the future.[71] All partner Churches would accept the Petrine ministry as the guarantor of the unity of the Church, while the Pope would respect the agreed-upon independence of the partner Churches. These and similar proposals are based on the conviction that an incomplete unity is more in accord with the Lord's command than the present disunity, and in the hope that they would be the first step towards fuller unity.

In one of his final reflections on the Church Rahner points the way for the Catholic Church itself to become more ecumenical and more catholic. Interpreting what he saw to be the fundamental theological significance of the Second Vatican Council, he says that both in the teaching of the Council and in the process of the Council itself the *Roman* Catholic Church began to become more the Roman *Catholic* Church, more of a genuinely universal and world Church.[72] Previously the Church had been worldwide in a geographical sense, but it 'exported' a European inculturation of the faith throughout the world. Rahner mentions what he sees as some of the first steps towards the inculturation of the Christian faith in other cultures.

First, in Vatican II bishops from many different cultures actively participated in a Council for the first time. Secondly, at this period the use of the vernacular was introduced into the Church's liturgy. Finally, the Council gave recognition to the value of the other world religions and to the presence of grace and the Holy Spirit among all peoples. He sees these moves as a 'qualitative leap', as epochal as the move of Christian faith from its origins in Jewish religion and culture into the Gentile world of Hellenistic culture.[73] For this reason the Council was not an end but a beginning, presenting a task and a challenge to the Church of the present and the future.

Notes

1   DV, no. 8.

2   In 'The Church of sinners', TI 6, p. 258, Rahner calls the Church 'the living body of Christ, animated by the Holy Spirit of God'.

3   See *The Church and the Sacraments* (*Quaestiones Disputatae* 9; Freiburg and New York: Herder, 1963/London: Burns & Oates, 1974), pp. 9–24; repr. in *Studies in Modern Theology* (Freiburg: Herder, London/Burns & Oates, 1965).

4   'The new image of the Church', TI 10, pp. 3–29.

5   Ibid., pp. 7–8, quoting from LG, no. 26.

6   Ibid., p. 10.

7   Ibid., p. 9.

8   Ibid., pp. 11–12.

9   *The Church and the Sacraments*, p. 18.

10   'Membership of the Church according to the teaching of Pius XII's encyclical "Mystici Corporis Christi"', TI 2, p. 83.

11   FC, pp. 322–3.

12   *The Church and the Sacraments*, p. 9.

13   See Rahner's treatment of original sin in FC, pp. 106–15.

14   'The new image of the Church', p. 14.

15   See 'Membership of the Church', pp. 1–88.

16   Ibid., p. 86.

17   See 'Anonymous Christians', TI 6, pp. 390–8, and 'Observations on the problem of the "Anonymous Christian"', TI 14, pp. 280–94.

18 'Christianity and the non-Christian religions', TI 5, pp. 115–34.

19 'On the importance of the non-Christian religions for salvation', TI 18, pp. 288–95.

20 'Atheism and implicit Christianity', TI 9, pp. 145–64.

21 'The Church of sinners', pp. 253–69.

22 Ibid., p. 259.

23 Ibid., p. 260.

24 Ibid.

25 Ibid., pp. 261–2.

26 *The Dynamic Element in the Church* (*Quaestiones Disputatae* 12; New York: Herder & Herder/London: Burns & Oates, 1964), p. 48.

27 Ibid.

28 Ibid., pp. 69–72.

29 FC, pp. 328–9.

30 Karl Rahner and Wilhelm Thüsing, *A New Christology* (London: Burns & Oates, 1980), pp. 18–22.

31 Ibid., pp. 23–4.

32 Ibid., p. 24.

33 Ibid., pp. 27–30.

34 'Reflections on the concept of "*Ius Divinum*" in Catholic thought', TI 5, pp. 219–43.

35 'On the relationship between the Pope and the college of bishops', TI 10, p. 55.

36 Ibid., pp. 69–70. See also on this question Karl Rahner and Joseph Ratzinger, *The Episcopate and the Primacy* (*Quaestiones Disputatae* 4; New York: Herder & Herder/London: Burns & Oates, 1962), repr. in *Studies in Modern Theology*.

37 'Aspects of the episcopal office', TI 14, p. 191.

38 Ibid., pp. 192–4. See also 'The episcopal office', TI 6, pp. 313–60.

39 See 'Theology and the Church's teaching authority after the Council', TI 9, pp. 83–100; 'The teaching office of the Church in the present-day crisis of authority', TI 12, pp. 3–30; 'The dispute concerning the Church's teaching office', TI 14, pp. 85–97; 'Magisterium and theology', TI 18, pp. 54–73.

40 'Magisterium and theology', p. 73.

41 'On the concept of infallibility in Catholic theology', TI 14, pp. 66–7.

42 Ibid., p. 71.

43   'The teaching of the Second Vatican Council on the diaconate', TI 10, pp. 231-2. See also 'On the diaconate', TI 12, pp. 61-80.

44   'How the priest should view his official ministry', TI 14, p. 202.

45   Ibid., pp. 207-8.

46   Ibid., pp. 217-19. See also 'The point of departure in theology for determining the nature of the priestly office', TI 12, pp. 31-8, and 'Theological reflections on the priestly image of today and tomorrow', TI 12, pp. 39-60.

47   'Women and the priesthood', TI 20, pp. 35-47.

48   'On bishops' conferences', TI 6, pp. 375-9.

49   Ibid., p. 380.

50   'On the theology of a "Pastoral Synod"', TI 14, p. 129.

51   *The Shape of the Church to Come* (New York: Seabury/London: SPCK, 1974), pp. 19-34.

52   Ibid., pp. 45-89.

53   Ibid., pp. 108-18.

54   'Basic observations on the subject of changeable and unchangeable factors in the Church', TI 14, p. 7.

55   'Observations on the factor of the charismatic in the Church', TI 12, p. 85.

56   Ibid., pp. 85-6.

57   Ibid., p. 87.

58   See 'The individual and the Church', *Nature and Grace* (London: Sheed & Ward, 1963/New York: Sheed & Ward, 1964), pp. 5-83.

59   *The Dynamic Element in the Church*, pp. 62-9.

60   'Observations on the factor of the charismatic in the Church', p. 88.

61   Ibid., pp. 92-3.

62   Ibid., pp. 94-7.

63   Ibid., p. 85.

64   'Dialogue in the Church', TI 10, pp. 103-21.

65   *Free Speech in the Church* (New York: Sheed & Ward, 1959).

66   'Membership of the Church', pp. 24-6.

67   'Some problems in contemporary ecumenism', TI 14, p. 251.

68   Ibid., pp. 252-3.

69   'Ecumenical theology in the future', TI 14, pp. 254-69.

70   Heinrich Fries and Karl Rahner, *Unity of the Churches: An Actual Possibility* (Philadelphia: Fortress, 1985), p. 1.

71   Ibid., pp. 36–8.

72   'Basic theological interpretation of the Second Vatican Council', TI 20, pp. 77–89.

73   Ibid., pp. 82–9.

7

Church and world

Karl Rahner's theology of the world follows from his understanding of grace and Jesus Christ. Christian faith is not about God's necessary or essential nature, but about God's free activity in the world, and most especially the historical event of God's revelation in Jesus Christ. In Jesus was revealed God's gracious presence in the world, and in the response of Jesus this presence achieved a union between God and the world so close that in the terms of the Council of Chalcedon, 'God and the world are never identical, but neither are they ever separate':

> But we have to say of the God whom we profess in Christ that he is exactly where we are, and only there is he to be found. If nevertheless he remains infinite, this does not mean that he is *also* still this, but means that the finite itself has received infinite depths. The finite is no longer in opposition to the infinite, but is that which the infinite himself has become, that in which he expresses himself . . .[1]

Christian faith, then, is about this relationship between God and the world, so that believing in God always includes believing something about the world.

Rahner points out that the Church's understanding of its relationship to the world has 'to some extent entered into a new stage with Vatican II'.[2] For in modern times the world has come to be understood in an historical sense, as the history of a single humanity. It is not merely an antecedent given, but is something being planned and shaped by humanity's own efforts. It was Karl Marx who first saw the world as something to be constructed by human beings themselves, as something to be changed rather than merely understood. The Second Vatican Council responded to this new vision in its Pastoral Constitution on the Church in the Modern World. There it understands the world as 'the theatre of man's history', and says that the Church 'is truly and intimately linked with mankind and its history' (nos. 1–2). 'World', then, does not carry the biblical connotation of being opposed to or hostile to God. It is the world God created good, fallen indeed into sin, but called to redemption and transformation.

This way of understanding the world stands in stark contrast to two other ways which have been operative throughout the history of the Church, explicitly or implicitly. The first Rahner calls 'integrism', which 'regards the world as mere material for the action and self-manifestation of the Church', and 'would integrate the world into the Church'.[3] An example would be the mediaeval theory of the 'two swords', which saw the secular sword 'as conferred by the Church to be employed in the service of the Church and its higher purposes'. Behind integrism lies the tacit but widespread assumption that from the moral principles taught by the Church and applied by its pastoral ministry a concrete prescription can be deduced, at least in principle, for every particular human action:

> The activity of the world in State, history and social life is then simply a realization of the Church's principles, and in fact an embodiment of the Church itself. The world would be the *corpus christianum* and nothing else.[4]

'Worldly matters' that were left to the 'princes' were regarded as of no consequence for salvation.

But this tacit assumption of integrism is false, because the human action that must be done here and now in some concrete situation cannot be derived wholly from the principles of the Gospel and natural law, although it must always respect these principles. Such secular actions are not for this reason morally unimportant or of no consequence for salvation and the coming of God's kingdom. Integrism is of the false opinion that at least in principle 'everything of importance for salvation belongs to the official Church' and so needs an 'ecclesiastical stamp'. All that is not of the Church is indifferent secular business. This opinion is especially false and dangerous today, when the world is seen as capable of being changed by human action which is of the utmost moral urgency and responsibility before God, but is not derived from nor directed by the Church. Integrism fails to see that 'Action regulated by the Church and Christian action which is genuinely human do not coincide'.[5]

Rahner calls the second false attitude towards the world 'esotericism', which regards the realm of the secular as simply indifferent for Christian faith and salvation. 'Flight from the world' is the only genuinely Christian attitude. Any affirmation of the world and its values is suspect unless explicitly motivated by a supernatural and religious intention. The sources of this attitude are many and varied:

> It may be based on a latent dualism which simply identifies the empirical aspect of the world with its sinfulness, so that remoteness from the world (its civilization, sexuality, self-development) is identified with detachment from sin and regarded undialectically as identical with greater closeness with God.[6]

It can be based on the view that what is genuinely moral and valid in God's sight is meta-historical and consists in an interior disposition devoid of concrete action in the world. The realm of the secular presents no positive task for the Christian and is to be abandoned in favour of a religious life lived exclusively with fellow esoterics. If for the integrist the world is ideally the Church, for the esoteric the world is ideally the monastery.

Vatican II's assertion of a 'true and intimate link' between the Church and the world rejects these two extremes of an integrist absorption of the world into the Church, which denies any difference between the two, and an esoteric rejection of the world, which denies any unity between Church and world. Rahner interprets this 'true and intimate link' as a differentiated unity between Church and world, with the difference between them emanating from a prior and radical unity, the unity of the history of God's gracious activity in bringing about his kingdom in the world.

The kingdom of God is not a purely interior or purely otherworldly reality coming hereafter 'to replace the world, its history and the outcome of its history'. Rather the kingdom 'is coming to be in the history of the world', and the Church as the community of faith in Jesus must continue his proclamation of this kingdom:

Above all, however, the Church is precisely its special fundamental sacrament, i.e., the eschatological and efficacious manifestation (sign) in redemptive history that in the unity, activity,
fraternity, etc. of the *world*, the kingdom of God is at hand.[7]

Since it is in the history of the world that the kingdom must come, the
Church exists not for itself, but for the kingdom and for the world.
Moreover, the proclamation of the Church, like that of Jesus, is not
only word, but also deed, 'the concrete fulfilment of an earthly task'
in carrying out the commandment to love one's neighbour in both an
individual and a social sense.

The more specific relationship between the Church and the world
and the concrete way of being 'sacrament' of the kingdom for the
world is different for the official institutional Church and for particular Christian communities and their individual members. The
former must 'proclaim the general principles of the dignity of man,
freedom, justice and love', as in Vatican II's Pastoral Constitution on
the Church in the Modern World, or in the papal encyclicals on social
justice and peace. It can also engage in more 'charismatic' kinds of
activity, such as the visits of John XXIII and Paul VI to the United
Nations. When these latter activities involve decisions and prescriptions which are not simply deductions from Christian principles, the
distinction between the two must not be obscured. In both cases the
Church must seek to influence the world by persuasion and not coer-
cion. Given the global and complex nature of today's social, economic and political situation, 'it is no longer possible for the Church
to give directly concrete prescriptions' in these areas, 'so that the limits
of the possibilities open to the official Church (free of integrist claims)
are plain'.[8]

The Church in the sense of individual Christians and Christian
groups has a different relationship to the world and a different way of
being sacrament than does the official Church. Their relationship is
based ultimately on the acceptance of the world by God through the
Incarnation of the Logos and the consequent graced nature of all
human reality and what this signifies:

It means the setting free of the world into independence, intrinsic
significance and autonomy. Closeness to God and the world's
own intrinsic reality are not inversely but directly proportionate.[9]

Involvement in the secular concerns of the world by individual
Christians and groups in a way that the official Church itself cannot

105

be involved, while not explicitly religious activity, is, nevertheless, Christian activity in a proper sense.[10] For the grace of Christ and the Spirit of Christ are not confined to a religious sphere nor to the official Church, but are at work in all of reality. Through the Incarnation the finite realm of the secular 'has received infinite depths'.

Moreover, as Rahner has emphasized against integrism, such secular activity by Christians is not merely applying Christian moral principles taught by the Church, as though specific courses of action could be deduced from them. It is also the discovery of what these principles really mean and require in a concrete situation here and now. This discovery can come through the investigations of secular sciences, so that to proclaim the kingdom in more than general and abstract terms the Church must not only teach the world, but also learn from it. Just as philosophy has been of service to the Church's theoretical concerns, so too can other sciences be of service to its practical concerns. Awareness of this also prevents the misconception that a 'Christian can be assured of the morality of his action, and of its accordance with God's will', merely by the fact that it is not in conflict with the material content of the norms taught by the Church.[11] Such a negative norm does not exhaust the positive responsibility of individual Christians in their service of the kingdom in the world.

When this positive attitude towards the secular is truly Christian, however, it is also aware of the other aspect of the world, the presence of sin and death. In the light of the cross the Christian knows that the world moves towards its goal 'through collapse, futility and the zero-point of death'. It is not tempted, therefore, to make of the world or any of its systems an absolute or an idol, but is mindful of the transcendence of God and that the kingdom is ultimately his gift. How this necessary detachment from the world and activity in and for the world are combined in the life of the individual Christian varies with different Christian vocations. But each in its own way will include 'readiness for renunciation', living by 'the spirit of the Sermon on the Mount' and the willingness 'to die with Christ'.[12]

Rahner's theology of the secular, therefore, is based on the conviction that because of the Incarnation the world 'is open towards a direct relation to God' in its 'depth dimension' and in its 'ultimate dynamism'.[13] When these dimensions of the world are touched, one is in touch with God's saving work:

A further point is that the dimension of the explicitly sacral, of the cult and of the preaching of the Gospel, is far from being

106

identical with the dimension in which salvation is achieved. This sphere in which salvation is achieved is identical with the sphere of human existence in general. As the mediatrix of salvation, therefore, it is quite impossible for the Church to adopt an attitude of indifference towards this total sphere of human existence . . .[14]

From this viewpoint, the modern process of secularization in which the world has asserted its autonomy and become more independent and separate from the Church is not necessarily a separation from 'God, his salvific grace or the historical realization of this in the world'.[15] Indeed, seen as a rejection of false integralism, secularization is 'right and just' by Christian standards.

As examples of this kind of secularization, Rahner mentions three areas of secular endeavour where a new and non-integralist relationship between the Church and the world has developed: 'in the humanities, in science and in society and politics'.[16] With regard to the humanities, he points out in his reflection on 'theology and the arts' that a work of art can be secular in content, and yet have religious and Christian significance. A painting by Rembrandt, for example, even if it is not religious in its thematic, objective content, can portray the human in such a way as to touch those depths where religious experience has its origins. Insofar as secular art is a genuine expression of the human and of the 'unfathomable mystery of things', it can evoke in the observer or listener experiences of the human which are open to the experience of God.[17]

Science, too, has become autonomous in this process of secularization. The Church is no longer the final arbiter of scientific questions, and theology is no longer the 'queen of the sciences', but 'a modest individual science' among others.[18] In this pluralism of the sciences, the Church and theology are both teacher and learner, and they still have 'a long time to spend in listening to the natural scientists' in order to gain an adequate knowledge of the contemporary world and the contemporary person to whom the message of salvation is addressed.[19] Not acknowledging the autonomy of secular knowledge and overstepping the boundaries of its competence was one reason for the supposed conflicts between science and religion in the past.[20]

Not only need religion and science not be in conflict, but in some ways the modern scientific worldview has a positive affinity to Christian teaching. For example, current scientific estimates of the immeasurable vastness of the universe reduce our planet and the human race to a marginal phenomenon of cosmic insignificance. But the dizzy sense of being lost in the cosmos can be the occasion for a genuine experience of finiteness and contingency and of God's incomprehensibility. In this light this view of the cosmos is 'more theological' than was the cosy geocentric view of earlier Christian ages.[21]

The third area of the secular mentioned by Rahner in which secularization calls for a new relationship between Church and world is that of society and politics. Having lost the direct involvement it had in this area in earlier, integralist times, the Church must not therefore retreat into a purely private sphere of religion in the fashion of esotericism. Such an individualistic and spiritualist view of revelation as pertaining only to the salvation of individual souls does not do justice to the kingdom Jesus preached. The changed circumstances of the modern, secular world do not lessen the Church's responsibility in social matters, but give it a new task, 'a task which might perhaps be characterized as "prophetic" '.[22] Rahner uses this term to describe the activity of the Church when it gives a concrete interpretation and practical application of its general moral principles to some particular situation, as distinguished from teaching the theoretical principles themselves as part of revelation. The Church does not have the same formal authority in the former as in the latter.

Nevertheless, the present age, and its desire to change the world and not just interpret it, calls for this kind of prophetic activity in the Church:

> Now the truth that stands revealed at this point is that the Church is fundamentally different from, and, for practical purposes must henceforward become something different from, the institution of truth merely at the level of the speculative reason ... Rather she must be the institution of the truth of the practical reason, the 'vision' and activity of which also belong to that institution which the revelation of God has created for itself. She is the people of God on pilgrimage, which is intended to, and wills to, imprint its eschatological hope upon the structures of worldly life ...[23]

The official Church itself must be the 'herald' of the prophetic impulse which is at work elsewhere in the Church. This new task of the official Church also implies a new task for theology:

Theology in the future, proceeding from the ground of the *practical* reason, will express the doctrines of the old theology of the theoretical reason in such a way that the theological as such will become a principle of action.[24]

This prophetic activity can take the form of social criticism wherein the Church opens up 'a perspective which transcends concrete social reality' and thereby shows it to be of 'relative value' and 'capable of change'.[25] In doing so it is carrying out the injunction of Vatican II that our eschatological hope in a new earth 'must not weaken but rather stimulate our concern' for the historical future of this earth.[26] As Rahner expresses it, 'The Christian attitude towards the absolute future which is God neither diminishes nor eliminates the responsibility it entails for a "this worldly" future, but rather imparts a radical dimension to it'.[27]

When Christians are involved in such secular concerns they are in touch not only with the affairs of this world, but also with God. For a person's 'immediacy to God and consequently his God-given status over the world and over himself is, must be and can be mediated by his world achievement and world task in his history of freedom'. Rahner sees a relationship of mutual conditioning and dependence between one's relationship to God and one's relationship to the finite world. Hence he says of the person who has been justified and set free by the grace of God's self-communication:

> Justification offers a person as endowed with absolute freedom for his world task a standpoint over the world from which he accomplishes and endures this task in ultimate freedom, and this world task itself even to the very limit of its apparent secularity is the mediation for the free acceptance of this immediacy to God . . . Grace, we might also say, has always and everywhere an incarnational structure; it descends into the world, but does not make this world unreal . . .[28]

One's world task is the visible embodiment and enactment of one's graced relationship to the invisible God.

Rahner applies this principle to love and hope which, as theological virtues as distinguished from moral virtues, have God and not a finite reality or value as their object. Nevertheless, because of the unity of the love of God and neighbour, when a person 'breaks out of the prison of egoism' and really loves his neighbour unconditionally, this love is itself the realization of the love of God, 'the event of the transcendence of the person towards God's immediacy'.[29] This is true even if the religious dimension, which is always present when love of neighbour reaches its real depths, is not explicit and thematic. This love is not mere feeling or sentiment, but is deed and action, and is not just interpersonal love, but also love in its social and collective dimension.

The same structure characterizes the theological virtue of hope. There is a unity between eschatological hope and inner-worldly hopes, the former being the ground and liberation of the latter. They are not identical, but mutually dependent.

> Only in the realization of intramundane hope can man realize his hope in the absolute future in genuine freedom. And only if he aspires in this theological hope to the intramundane goals of his history, continually to be seized on creatively in hope, does he gain the right attitude to his desired intramundane goals and tasks.[30]

This right attitude is freedom from the need to absolutize or make an idol of any intramundane present or future, a freedom from the world for the world.

But in thus relativizing all worldly realities in the light of God's absolute future, the theological virtue of hope does not make one indifferent to these realities. This relativization also has a positive side:

> It makes us free for other possibilities in the present world. It relativizes the here and now existing (sometimes positive) realities of life and society; it makes us free and open for future possibilities of history and society; . . . it is a critique and rejection of a false, merely static conservatism, defending only things as they exist, without courage for risk or for any experiment which cannot be adequately calculated at every turn.[31]

Being open in hope to God's absolute future is not an interior attitude, but must be embodied in and mediated by one's openness to the future here and now. The creation of a more human future 'is not something optional for the Christian, but is the means by which he prepares himself, in actuality and not merely in theory, for God's absolute future'.[32]

Rahner is aware that this change in the Church's attitude and relationship to the social and political realm of the secular world has its dangers and exaggerated forms not only outside, but also inside the Church. They manifest themselves in the desire to reduce the Gospel message to its 'secular meaning', and to reduce Jesus to being merely an ethical teacher or a social revolutionary. He calls this 'pure horizontalism', and sees its roots today not only in a legitimate concern and sense of responsibility for the world, but also in an excessive and illegimate 'demythologizing' of the Gospel, and in the rationalistic mentality engendered by a scientific and technical worldview. The solution to the danger of such radical horizontalism is not an equally dangerous 'verticalism', but a genuinely incarnational understanding of grace and salvation which sees the intrinsic and necessary relationship of mutual dependence between the 'religious' and the 'secular' in Christian life.[33]

It is in this sense that Rahner insists that Christianity cannot allow itself to become an ideology among other ideologies in the world. He uses the term 'ideology' in the sense of 'a fundamental closure in face of the "wholeness" of reality, one which turns a partial aspect into an absolute'.[34] He distinguishes between 'ideologies of immanence' which turn 'certain finite areas of our experiential world into absolutes and regard their structures as the law of reality as such', and those of 'transmanence', a kind of supernaturalism which totalizes something ultimate at the expense of the relative rights of the penultimate. A third form is the 'ideology of transcendence' which tries to surmount the first two by simply staying 'open' and not committed to anything definite.

Now it must be granted that Christianity and the Church have not always avoided ideological thinking in these various senses. But because the God in whom Christians believe is the incomprehensible mystery whom we do not 'grasp', but who lays hold of us, God cannot be made part of any system, including theological or religious systems. Moreover, since Christianity in its historical dimension is the sign of God's universal saving will and activity, it is not exclusive but inclusive. Nor can it be identified with any single social, economic or political system claiming to be the absolute solution to secular problems. For all of these reasons Christianity is not an ideological system and must not allow itself to be used as one.[35]

A final question about the material, secular world which Rahner addresses is whether it is to have any part in what Christians believe is going to be the final consummation of all things. Is the secular world and secular history included within the hope of Christian eschatology? An earlier way of thinking tended to see the world as merely the stage upon which individual human beings worked out their individual salvation. History provided the situations and the material for the exercise of Christian virtues by which salvation was attained. But the world and history themselves had no final or ultimate validity. The kingdom of God was thought to be coming 'to replace the world, its history and the outcome of its history'. For both theological and philosophical reasons Rahner recommends a new and more inclusive eschatology.

Commenting on the use of the term 'new earth' in the Second Vatican Council's Pastoral Constitution on the Church in the Modern World, he poses the theological question whether 'new' is to be understood in the sense of a different earth to replace the old, or in the sense of a 'renewed' and 'transformed' earth.[36] In either case it is to be understood as the eschatological gift of God, and not merely the outcome of worldly progress. But the Council's use of the phrases 'transformation of the world' (no. 38) and 'transformation of all things' (no. 39) justifies interpreting 'new' in the second sense. The world and human history will finally endure and will be radically transformed. By saying this we both endow the present with radical importance and at the same time remain open to God's future.[37] Among other reasons for seeing the history which is now in the process of being constructed by human endeavour as of ultimate value and significance, is the need to counter the Marxist criticism that Christianity devalues the present and human efforts to change it.

The same interpretation of the final destiny of the world and history is also recommended for philosophical reasons. The issue from this point of view is how one conceives the relationship between human beings and the material environment in which they exist, and how one conceives the basic relationship between spirit and matter.[38] Rahner postulates a real unity and mutual interrelationship between spirit and matter:

The physical world is not merely the outward stage upon which the history of the spirit, to which matter is basically alien, is played out, such that it tends as its outcome to quit this stage as swiftly as possible in order really to achieve full and complete spirituality in a world beyond that of matter. In a metaphysical interpretation matter is considered rather as that other factor which is necessary, in which and upon which alone *a finite and creaturely* spirituality can be *precisely that which* it is of its nature, and can bring this to its fullness.[39]

A spiritual creature at the finite level is inconceivable without the materiality which is the medium and expression of its self-fulfilment. Spirit and matter are essentially different, but precisely as the metaphysical principles of a single being. In this light the whole evolutionary process of matter can be viewed as tending towards its self-presence in spiritual existence.

While, then, it must be said that the material world considered in itself cannot reach a fulfilment or consummation in the sense of producing its own lasting result, considered in its intrinsic unity with spirit it is an essential part of the latter's consummation:

> Matter . . . must be thought of not as a condition for spirit, or as something necessary for it to be brought to its fullness such that once its consummation has been achieved it is simply cast aside as a means which has become superfluous or as a transitory stage through which it has passed. It endures as an intrinsic element of the spirit and of its history even in its consummation.[40]

Insofar as the material world is carried beyond itself in its self-transcendence to spirit, it achieves in the consummation of the latter its own consummation. The fact that we cannot imagine or conceive the nature of this final state of its existence is no argument against it. The material world and its history, then, are no mere 'launching pad' which is left behind, but should be included as an integral part of our faith and hope in the 'resurrection of the body'.[41]

Notes

1   FC, p. 226.

2   'Church and World', SM I, p. 346.

3   Ibid., p. 349.

4   Ibid.

5   Ibid., p. 350.

6   Ibid.

7   Ibid., p. 348.

8   Ibid., pp. 351–2.

9   Ibid., p. 353.

10   Ibid., p. 352.

11   Ibid.

12 Ibid., pp. 353–5.

13 Ibid., p. 353.

14 'The function of the Church as a critic of society', TI 12, pp. 238–9.

15 'Theological reflections on the problem of secularization', TI 10, pp. 318–19.

16 Ibid., p. 322.

17 'Theology and the arts', *Thought* LVII, no. 224 (March 1982), pp. 17–29.

18 'On the relationship between natural science and theology', TI 19, pp. 19–20.

19 'Theology as engaged in an interdisciplinary dialogue with the sciences', TI 13, p. 92.

20 'Natural science and reasonable faith', TI 21, pp. 24–7.

21 Ibid., pp. 48–51.

22 'Theological reflections on the problem of secularization', p. 330.

23 Ibid., pp. 335–6.

24 'Karl Rahner: an interview', *America* 123, no. 13 (31 October 1970), p. 358.

25 'The function of the Church as a critic of society', p. 235.

26 GS, no. 39.

27 'The question of the future', TI 12, p. 191.

28 'Justification and world development from a Catholic viewpoint', TI 18, p. 269.

29 Ibid., pp. 269–70. See also 'Reflections on the unity of the love of neighbour and the love of God', TI 6, pp. 231–49.

30 Ibid., p. 271.

31 'Theological justification of the Church's development work', TI 20, pp. 71–2.

32 'Christian humanism', TI 9, p. 201.

33 See 'The Church's commission to bring salvation and the humanization of the world', TI 14, pp. 295–313.

34 'Ideology and Christianity', TI 6, p. 44.

35 Ibid., pp. 47–58.

36 'The theological problems entailed in the idea of the "new earth" ', TI 10, p. 266.

37 Ibid., pp. 269–70.

38 See 'The unity of spirit and matter in the Christian understanding of faith', TI 6, pp. 153–77.

39 'Immanent and transcendent consummation of the world', TI 10, p. 285.

40 Ibid., pp. 288-9.

41 'Natural science and reasonable faith', p. 54.

8

The Christian vocation

It follows from Karl Rahner's understanding of grace as universally offered to all people through Christ, and of the Church as the visible, historical sign of this grace, that being a Christian and a member of the Church does not separate one from those who are not, but gives expression to one's union with them. Christian identity is not exclusive and divisive, but inclusive and unitive:

> The basic and ultimate thrust of Christian life consists not so much in the fact that a Christian is a special instance of mankind in general, but rather in the fact that a Christian is simply man as he is. But he is a person who accepts without reservations the whole of concrete human life with all of its adventures, its absurdities and its incomprehensibilities.[1]

Neither does this identity separate the Christian from the larger world of secular experience, for it is there that the Christian vocation must be lived. For being a Christian is not a separate compartment of life, but is that which animates and focuses the whole.

Understanding the Church as a sign of what is true of the whole human family rather than as a special and privileged enclave within it changes the meaning of Church membership, but does not lessen its importance. Rahner points to this new meaning and importance in his reflections on baptism as the initiation rite which makes a person a member of the Church. It is not enough to think of the Church 'as the dispenser of the means of grace for the individual's salvation',[2] means which are not to be had without the Church:

But the meaning and purpose of the church is not merely and exclusively to make it possible and to make it easier for the sum of many individuals to find their individual salvation. For it could indeed be regarded as useful and important for this purpose, but not as unconditionally necessary; this purpose is often achieved without any tangible intervention of the church . . .[3]

Although incorporation into the Church through baptism is in fact, then, a means of grace and salvation for the individual, baptism must also have 'a positive content and significance for the individual' beyond this.

For even though grace and salvation are possible without the Church, there is one thing that is not possible without the Church:

That the grace of God in Christ be present in the world as an event, as an ongoing event with historical tangibility and with incarnational corporeality. Anyone who receives grace in baptism by being incorporated into the church . . . necessarily receives along with the grace of the church a share in, and the mandate and capacity for participating in, this function of the church to be the historical tangibility of God's grace in the world.[4]

Baptism, then, does not just concern individual salvation, but is a community rite, an initiation into the community and into its reality as sign. Insofar as membership in this community and belonging to it is the first and most immediate effect of the sacrament, one 'is appointed by baptism to be a messenger of the word, a witness to the truth, and a representative of the grace of Christ in the world'.

This meaning of Church membership is also emphasized by that part of the initiation rite which was separated off and came to be known as 'confirmation'. Though now separated in time from baptism, it retains its meaning as part of one's inititiation into the community. This part of the rite, too, highlights the active nature of Church membership:

Confirmation . . . emphasizes the social and functional aspect of the baptized insofar as he is empowered by the communication of the Holy Spirit. It is the sacrament of giving witness to the faith, of charismatic fullness, of the mission of one sealed with the

117

Spirit to give witness to the world so that it will become subject to the Lordship of God.[5]

Through confirmation one shares in the Church's grace and mission for the transformation of the world. All who are incorporated into the Body of Christ receive the one Spirit who animates it, and it is the Spirit who decides the particular charism and mission for each member. But whatever the charism, through Church membership one is always not just a passive recipient of grace from the community, but also an active participant in its life as the sign of grace.

Prior, then, to any further differentiation in the Church between laity and clergy, baptism and confirmation are the 'sacramental consecration' by which 'every Christian in the Church has been authorized and empowered for the task of actively co-operating in the work of the Church both interiorly and exteriorly'.[6] This means that what laity and clergy have in common is more fundamental than what differentiates them. For though only the ordained minister can administer the Eucharist, 'he achieves the fullness of his personal Christian life in virtue of the fact not that he imparts, but rather that he receives this sacrament like every other Christian'.[7] Indeed, it is possible for a lay person to have a task of more importance for the mission of the Church:

> For it can be the case that a free charism in the Church, such as a layman too can be favoured with, may in practice be of greater significance for the salvation of mankind and of the world than the exercise of an institutional, official or even sacramental authority.[8]

Because the layman remains involved in the secular affairs of the world, 'it is because of him that the Church is present precisely *there*', and it is there that 'he has the responsibility of being a sign in the world and to the world of the eternal reality of salvation'.[9]

Reflecting further on baptism and confirmation as the two moments of the Church's initiation rite, Rahner asks why the two rites are called sacramental actions. He has already employed this term to understand Jesus Christ as the sacrament or symbol of God's gracious presence in the world, and the Church as the sacrament or symbol of the ongoing historical presence of Jesus Christ. In both instances a sacrament is understood as a real symbol in the sense of a visible, tangible embodiment and manifestation in which the symbolized becomes present.[10] Such a real symbol is not merely the 'subsequent notification of something that has already taken place and is in being', or the extrinsic announcement of a 'state of affairs that is quite unaffected' by the symbol.[11] Rather the symbol is actually the medium which enables the symbolized to become present, and in this sense is a cause of this presence. Rahner calls this 'symbolic causality', and it is as symbolic causes rather than as efficient causes that he understands sacraments to effect what they signify and to effect precisely by signifying and symbolizing.

Understanding baptism and confirmation as sacramental activities in this sense, they are symbolic actions in which God's justifying and sanctifying love becomes manifest and present for a particular individual. By making this individual a member of the visible Church, the sacramental action says and proclaims what this individual actually is, a child of God and brother of Jesus Christ. Through the sacramental action one becomes in a fuller and manifest way what one already is. Moreover, Catholic Tradition teaches that sacramental actions are 'infallible' signs of grace and effect grace *ex opere operato*. This means that the word of God's love and forgiveness to which the sacramental action of the Church gives voice and which it makes audible is spoken freely by God and purely on God's own initiative, and that in the history of Jesus Christ this word has become irrevocable and unambiguous.[12] God's offer of grace is not dependent on the subjective merit of the minister or the recipient, but is *sola gratia*. It must, however, be freely heard and accepted in faith to be fruitful, and this human side of the sacramental dialogue is what the Tradition calls the *opus operantis*. Grace is a relationship which requires freedom on both sides.[13]

Because sacramental actions are unfailing signs of God's grace they can also be understood as the supreme instance of God's word in the Church. In the past theology has tended to separate word and sacrament as two different realities, but when understood as symbolic actions sacraments also have the character of word. In his theology of the word Rahner distinguishes a variety of ways in which God's word is uttered in the Church. The notion of God's word like that of human words in general is intrinsically variable, and includes the word of Scripture, the word of proclamation and the word of teaching and doctrine. In its full and original sense the word of God is not a word about God, but God speaking, God expressing himself and becoming present through self-communication. Such a word has the character of an 'event' and is an 'exhibitive' word. It does not merely convey information about God:

Rather it is to be conceived of as an exhibitive word, a word that renders present. It is in it and through it that the reality designated is first and foremost given, and, moreover, in a relationship of mutual conditioning of such a kind that the word is constituted by the reality which thereby comes to be, and the reality comes to be in that, and because, it reveals itself in this way.[14]

In this light, sacramental actions can be seen as 'the supreme human and ecclesial stage of the word in all its dimensions which has been uttered in the church as such'.[15]

If sacramental actions are the supreme instance of God speaking his word in and through the Church, it is in the celebration of the Eucharist that this is most fully realized both for the individual Christian and for the Church as a whole. The Eucharist is 'the sacrament of the church as such in a very radical sense', for the institution of the Lord's Supper 'is of decisive importance for the founding of the church and for the self-understanding of Jesus as the mediator of salvation'.[16] The celebration of the Eucharist has its foundation in the Last Supper where in his own words Jesus gives his 'body' and his 'blood' to be eaten and drunk under the appearance of receiving bread and wine. The content and meaning of this action are fraught with significance for our understanding of both Jesus and the Church:

> The idea of death is of decisive importance: Jesus accepts his fate consciously and connects it with the central content of his preaching. Moreover, Jesus understands this meal in an eschatological way as an anticipation of the joy of the final and definitive banquet. Finally, at this meal with Jesus the idea of community is constitutive, that is, the union of Jesus with his friends and the foundation of the community of these friends among themselves.[17]

The identity of the gifts with Jesus expresses his acceptance of a violent death in free obedience, thereby establishing a new covenant.

The Eucharistic celebration of the Church is always a meal insofar as the body and blood of Christ are present as food,[18] and by sharing this meal the Christian is more deeply incorporated into the one Body of Christ. At the same time the bloody sacrifice of Jesus on the cross becomes present when he is remembered in the repetition of the Lord's Supper at his own command: 'Do this in memory of me'.

For 'it is the flesh and blood of the *suffering* and *dying* servant of God *as* sacrificed and poured out for many which become present'.[19] This Eucharist which is both meal and sacrifice is also a 'giving thanks' to God who accepted the sacrifice of Jesus and raised him from the dead. The mystery which becomes present in the Eucharistic word and symbol, then, is the total and single mystery of the redemptive life, death and resurrection of Jesus, and hence it is the central sacramental action of the Church's life.

The 'effect' of the Eucharist, therefore, must be seen from two points of view. There is, first of all, the effect for and in the individual:

> . . . the effect through which the individual receives his personal participation in the life of Jesus Christ, and also receives the grace to live out this participation in a 'Christian life' in the strictest sense, that is, the very life of Jesus Christ in love, obedience and gratitude to the Father, a life which represents gratitude and patience.[20]

But there is also and especially a social and ecclesial effect:

> In the Eucharist the gratuitous and irrevocable salvific will of God for all men becomes present, tangible and visible *in* this world insofar as through the Eucharist the tangible and visible community of believers is fashioned into *that* sign which does not only point to some possible grace and salvific will of God, but rather *is* the tangibility and the permanence of this grace and this salvation.[21]

Because the Eucharist is the sacrament of the most radical and real presence of the Lord in the world, it is 'fullest actualization of the essence of the church'.

It is clear in Rahner's treatment of the Eucharist as well as baptism and confirmation that his understanding of sacramental actions is not so much that one part of the Church 'administers' sacraments to another part for their own individual benefit. Rather in sacramental actions the community actualizes its own nature as the sacrament of grace, thus deepening the community's life of grace and that of the individual Christian through association with the community. Sacramental actions are intrinsically social, public and in this sense liturgical. At the time of the Reformation it became a controversial question how many such sacramental actions were legitimate in the

Church, and Catholics and Protestants divided over this issue. Both sides based this legitimacy on the fact that Jesus had instituted sacraments, but the question was how many.

Rahner considers this 'positivistic' approach to the question unnecessary, and, in view of our knowledge of the historical Jesus and what he did or did not explicitly institute, impossible in any case. Contemporary exegesis does not support the arguments used by either Catholics or Protestants at the time of the Reformation.[22] Both sides have drawn closer together in the sense that they both need a new point of departure for deciding this question. Rahner's point of departure is to see the sacraments as entailed in the institution of the Church:

> ... we can say that the origin or the institution of the sacraments has to be understood, and also *can* be understood, in a way which is analogous to the institution of the church itself by Jesus. The sacramentality of the church's basic activity is implied by the very essence of the church as the irreversible presence of God's salvific offer in Christ. This sacramentality is interpreted by the church in the seven sacraments . . .[23]

For Rahner the Church's 'principle of interpretation' lies in certain 'existentielly decisive situations in human life' or key moments which call for an engagement and action by the Church in which she actualizes the fullness of her nature as sign of grace for one of her members.[24]

One such situation lies in the fact that the new life in Christ begun in baptism and renewed in the celebration of the Eucharist is always 'the threatened life of a sinner'. Through either serious or slight sins the Christian acts in contradiction to his vocation and to the community to which he belongs. Hence God's word of forgiveness must be heard time and time again, a word which can never be taken for granted, but is always the miracle of God's love and mercy.

> When this word of God's forgiveness is addressed to an individual baptized person upon the confession of his guilt by a representative of the church who has been expressly designated for this, we call this event of God's word of forgiveness the reception of the sacrament of penance.[25]

God's word of forgiveness is not only the consequence, but also the presupposition of a person's conversion to God in trust and contrition. The expression of this word in the sacrament of penance is an integral part of a Christian's ongoing and ever deeper conversion to God which does not reach its fulfilment until death.[26]

In his historical studies into the origins and development of the sacrament of penance,[27] Rahner discovered what he called 'forgotten truths' about this sacrament which are still important for us today. Among them is the understanding of sin as being against the Church as well as against God, and therefore reconciliation through and with the Church is the sign of reconciliation with God.[28] It is in this context that he understands the Matthaean phrase 'binding and loosing'. The former refers to the distancing of the sinner from the Church upon the admission of guilt, thereby making visible what has in fact occurred through sin. The 'loosing' is the visible acceptance back into full communion with the Church upon the completion of penance.[29]

Another forgotten truth is the theory of Thomas Aquinas that the absolution of the priest and the acts of the penitent *together* constitute the sacramental sign of penance. This brings out two important truths. The first is that sacramental and personal elements are intimately interwoven in this sacrament, and in Christian life in general. Secondly, a sacrament is the self-actualization of the Church not only in the one who administers it, but also in the one who receives it. Together they are the Church in the sacramental action.[30]

There is a second sense and a second situation in which the life of a Christian is a 'threatened life'. It is the situation of serious sickness and the approach of death. This moment in which the sick person must face in loneliness the darkness and mystery of death is a moment which calls for the visible presence of the community of hope. The grace of its invincible faith and hope in the dying and rising Jesus must become manifest in the sacramental prayers and anointing of the person summoned to die and rise with him. In this sacramental rite the Church gives witness to its eschatological hope and makes God's gracious, forgiving and healing love present in its saving power over life and death.[31]

There are two final situations for which the Church has developed sacramental actions. They both involve the choice of states in life, and as states in which a person accepts an all-encompassing role and function in a human and Christian community, they represent decisive, existential moments in that person's life. The first is the sacrament of matrimony in which two members of the Christian community are united in a lifelong commitment of love and fidelity.

Marriage in general is by its very nature a sign, a sign of the love and union of the two parties which comes to expression at the social level of married life. If one considers in addition the unity which exists between the love of God and love of neighbour, marriage by its very nature has something to do with God. If one considers further that in the present order of God's universal offer of grace every morally good act is also a saving act, then married love always includes grace and opens out to the immediacy of God himself. Such love is in one sense exclusive, but at the same time if it is genuine love it reaches out to others as well.[32]

It is within this larger context that Rahner considers the sacramentality of Christian marriage. Since the Church, like marriage, is a sign of God's love, married love in the Church is one of the ways this love becomes actual and the Church becomes a real sign. Married love is formative and constitutive of the Church, and the union of the partners is a self-actualization of the Church's own essence. Marriage and family are the smallest Christian community, the smallest cell in the Body of Christ, but they are a genuine community in which the Church is present. Hence the assertion in Ephesians (5:22–33) that the marriage bond is an image of the union between Christ and the Church. Rahner sees the real point of the passage not in the parallel drawn between Christ and the husband on the one hand, and between the Church and the wife on the other, implying in both cases the subordination of one to the other. Rather the real theological point is that the unity of love between the partners is an image and representation of the union of Christ and the Church.[33]

The other state of life which is accompanied by a sacramental action on the part of Church is the conferral of certain ministries and offices through the sacrament of orders. It is clear that certain basic offices are constitutive of the Church, and that it is essential for the Church to hand them on along with the powers that accompany them. But why is the act by which the Church does this also a conferral of grace and hence can be called a sacrament? It is clear from the early struggle against Donatism that a Church office retains its validity and the office-holder retains his power even if the latter is a sinner and exercises his office in a sinful way. The validity of a sacrament is not dependent on the holiness of the minister.

However true this is, it cannot express the whole truth about the relationship between office and holiness in the Church. It follows from the nature of the Church as the holy Church that it is not a matter of indifference whether office is exercised in a holy way. An office that would be totally bereft of holiness throughout the whole of its exercise in all of its members would be incompatible with a holy Church. For it would assume that the holiness of the members of the Church was not dependent on the right exercise of office. It is not the administration of an individual sacrament that is dependent on the holiness of the minister, but the very existence and continuation of sacraments in the Church that is so dependent. Hence such offices are conferred through the sacrament of orders which is also a conferral of grace for the sanctification of the office-holder.[34]

Besides the two permanent states of life in the Church which are entered into through sacramental actions, there is also the life of the vows in the Church's religious orders. Based on the 'evangelical counsels' of poverty, chastity and obedience, it represents a particular way of living out the common Christian vocation given by baptism.[35] Since the Second Vatican Council it has been emphasized that all members of the Church are called to a mature Christian life in the spirit of the Gospel, and that religious are not distinguished from others by being the 'better' or the 'real' Christians.[36] Nevertheless, through the renunciation of genuine human values such as marriage and family life for the sake of the kingdom, the religious orders constitute a sign within the Church that it lives by faith and hope in God and his promise, and not in the power of this world. Moreover, the various services performed by the orders for God's people bear witness in action and in deed to God's love for the world.

In all seven of these sacramental actions Rahner's emphasis is on their social, ecclesial nature. One receives grace through association with the community which is the sign of grace, and the sacramental actions deepen this association. But in showing the common theological meaning shared by all seven sacraments, he does not deny that when compared with one another the seven 'differ very essentially in importance among themselves'.[37] Insofar as Catholic theology sees the centrality of baptism and Eucharist as the principal sacraments, and Protestant theology sees the possibility of other and analogous sacramental words in the Church, the way is open to resolving the Reformation controversy about the number of sacraments in the Church.

By analogy with the use of the term 'ascending' Christology, Rahner's theology of the sacraments can also be described as an ascending theology. It is a different way of 'experiencing the sacraments', and one he thinks is called for in the contemporary Church.[38] It differs from experiencing the sacraments, particularly the Eucharist, as 'an isolated encounter with God' which takes place within sacred precincts which one enters by leaving the secular world of everyday life behind. It is only within these precincts that one achieves closeness and union with God and Jesus Christ, whose actions 'touch the individual as it were from without'. Through this encounter people are strengthened, although for the most part in a transitory and peripheral way, for their return to the secular world and its remoteness from God. But when the religious realm is experienced in this way as separate from everyday life, it can also strike many people as having little to do with 'real reality' or 'real life' and then it ceases to be a genuine force in our everyday world.[39]

Rahner describes the other way of experiencing the Eucharist as involving a twofold movement:

> . . . an intellectual and spiritual movement of the sacramental event outwards to take effect in the 'world', and backwards in a spiritual movement leading from the world to the sacrament.[40]

If 'the world is permeated by the grace of God' and sacraments are specific events and symbols of this grace, God's action need not be understood as impinging upon the world intermittently and penetrating it from without, then receding until another such action is performed. It can be seen rather as rising out of the innermost roots of his creation wherever God's offer of grace is accepted throughout the whole length and breadth of human existence.

It is this whole fullness of life which must come to expression in the sacramental event, not a distilled and remote religiosity. For it must be said of the event of grace:

> It takes place not as a special phenomenon, as one particular process *apart from* the rest of human life. Rather it is quite simply the ultimate depths and the radical dimension of all that which the spiritual creature experiences, achieves and suffers in all those areas in which it achieves its own fullness, and so in its laughter and its tears, in its taking of responsibility, in its loving, living and dying . . .[41]

Christians find in Jesus of Nazareth the clearest manifestation and triumph of this grace, and in him we are all united in our common lot. It is here in the 'liturgy of the world' and its drama that the real history of grace is taking place, and this liturgy must come to expression in sacramental actions.

God is worshipped not only in Jerusalem and the temple, but everywhere 'in spirit and in truth'. It is from the liturgy of the world that the sacraments must draw their energy and their strength lest they become empty ritual. The drama of Golgotha is worldwide and lasts until the end of time, for all people and the Son of Man are one in their history and their destiny. The cross of Jesus that is remembered and proclaimed is also a present fact: the tears of Jesus are present in those who mourn today, and his blood is present in those who suffer and die today. Communion with the body of the Lord is communion with his whole body, and compassion for him embraces all his members.[42]

When the sacraments in general, and the Eucharist in particular, are understood as signs in this comprehensive sense, the latter can indeed be called the 'supreme moment' and the 'source' of life for the Christian, but in a 'conditional sense':

> It is a 'supreme moment' only to the extent that he allows God to determine *which particular* moment of his life, and under which particular 'forms', whether sacred or profane, he will encounter in his life that decisive moment, that sidereal hour, in which his ultimate self-surrender to God is really achieved for him . . .[43]

It is a 'source' only to the extent that he knows that if 'he opens his heart in faith, hope and love, the whole of his existence will be permeated throughout as a land from the depths of which flow the waters of eternal life'. When, then, in technical language the *res sacramenti*, that is, the reality designated by the sign of the Eucharist, is identical with the whole unfolding history of the world in which Jesus is the supreme moment, the Eucharist will epitomize the twofold movement in which sacraments embrace the reality of the world and bring to expression its deepest truth.

It is by being part of the liturgy of the world that the Christian will discover what Rahner calls 'the mysticism of everyday things'.[44] Indeed, given the new situation of the Christian where Christian faith is not taken for granted as part of culture, nor supported by social structures and attitudes, he thinks that 'the Christian of the future will be a mystic' if there are going to be genuine Christians at all.[45] By this he does not mean the mysticism of unusual parapsychological phenomena, but the experience of God and his Spirit that arises out of one's own Christian life of faith, hope and love. In all genuine believing, hoping and loving there takes place that self-transcendence, that losing of self, wherein one finds God as the innermost depths of one's experience. Here God is known not by indoctrination from without, but from within Christian experience itself. Mystical experience in the more specialized sense is but one particular form in which this self-transcendence takes place, and is the paradigm and exemplar of what occurs in all Christian life in different ways.

But whatever form this life takes, Rahner singles out several features that should characterize the life of every Christian.[46] Christian life is characterized by a freedom that can be open to all of God's creation without turning anything into an idol. It is characterized by a hope which makes this freedom possible because it is a hope in God and his power, and not in one's own or the world's power. Because of this hope a Christian can accept the pluralism of existence and the multiplicity of values without trying to reduce everything to a single system and a single value. Such freedom and hope make the Christian a person of responsibility who accepts the pain and ambiguity of moral struggle for a better self and a better world.

But through it all Christian life is characterized by realism, indeed, a 'pessimistic' realism. For the Christian knows that the path to fulfilment lies through death:

> Christianity is the religion which recognizes a man who was nailed to a cross and on it died a violent death as a sign of victory and as a realistic expression of human life, and it has made this its own sign.[47]

Hence the Christian who lives by this sign knows that he or she will be spared nothing, but also knows that the cross is prelude to resurrection and eternal life.

This is the single Christian vocation within the many Christian callings as laity or clergy, as married, single or religious. There is a single norm by which they are all measured: 'Those who love the most, believe the most, and hope the most, are the best, the most excellent Christians'.[48]

Notes

1 FC, p. 402.

2 *The Church and the Sacraments* (*Quaestiones Disputatae* 9; Freiburg: Herder, 1963/London: Burns & Oates, 1974), p. 9.

3 FC, p. 416.

4   Ibid.

5   Ibid., p. 417.

6   'The sacramental basis for the role of the layman in the Church', TI 8, p. 54.

7   Ibid., p. 70.

8   Ibid., p. 73.

9   Ibid., pp. 61, 63.

10 See 'The theology of the symbol', TI 4, pp. 221–52.

11 *The Church and the Sacraments*, p. 38.

12 Ibid., p. 32.

13 See 'Personal and sacramental piety', TI 2, pp. 109–33.

14 'What is a sacrament?', TI 14, pp. 140–1, note 10.

15 Ibid., p. 137. See also 'The world and the Eucharist', TI 4, pp. 253–81.

16 FC, pp. 424–5.

17 Ibid., p. 425.

18 See 'The presence of Christ in the sacrament of the Lord's Supper', TI 4, pp. 287–311.

19 FC, pp. 425–6.

20 Ibid., p. 426. See also 'The Eucharist and our daily lives', TI 7, pp. 211–26; and 'The Eucharist and suffering', TI 3, pp. 161–70.

21 FC, pp. 426–7.

22 'What is a sacrament?', pp. 135–6.

23 FC, p. 413.

24 Ibid., pp. 412–13. See also *The Church and the Sacraments*, p. 41.

25 FC, p. 422.

26 See 'The meaning of frequent confession of devotion', TI 3, pp. 177–89.

27 See TI 15, the entire volume of which is devoted to the topic 'Penance in the early Church'.

28 *The Church and the Sacraments*, p. 94.

29 'Forgotten truths concerning the sacrament of penance', TI 2, pp. 136–52.

30 Ibid., pp. 153–62.

31 See FC, pp. 423–4; *The Church and the Sacraments*, pp. 112–15.

32 'Marriage as a sacrament', TI 10, pp. 203–9.

33   Ibid., pp. 218–21.

34   FC, pp. 417–19.

35   See 'On the evangelical counsels', TI 8, pp. 133–67.

36   'The Religious life', *The Practice of Faith* (New York: Cross-road, 1983), p. 200; (London: SCM, 1985), p. 178.

37   'What is a sacrament?', p. 148.

38   'Considerations on the active role of the person in the sacramental event', TI 14, p. 163.

39   Ibid., pp. 162–5.

40   Ibid., p. 162.

41   Ibid., p. 167.

42   Ibid., pp. 169–74.

43   Ibid., pp. 174–5.

44   *The Practice of Faith* (1983), pp. 69–70; (1985), p. 62.

45   Ibid., p. 22 (1983, 1985).

46   See FC, pp. 402–11.

47   Ibid., p. 404.

48   *The Practice of Faith* (1983), p. 200; (1985), p. 178.

9

Ethics and eschatology

Although Karl Rahner was not a moral theologian, the principles
he employed in systematic theology have implications for moral
and ethical questions. Among these should be mentioned, first, his
understanding of human nature, which implies a renewed understanding of what is meant by the natural law. Secondly, his understanding of the human person calls for the development of an
individual or existential ethic along with an essential ethic. Finally,
his understanding of the relationship between God and the world
has implications for the relationship between the theological
virtues of faith, hope and charity which have God as their object,
and the moral virtues which are concerned with finite values. We
have already seen examples of this in the relationship between the
love of God and love of neighbour and between eschatological
hope and secular hopes.

In order to understand grace as an intrinsic part of human existence without prejudice to its supernatural character, and in order
to understand the hypostatic union as an intrinsic potentiality of
this graced human existence, Rahner employed a concept of human
nature that is essentially open to God's free disposition. God
created human nature as a potentiality, as an obediential potency
(*potentia oboedientialis*) to be determined by God's free action in
history summoning it towards its goal and destiny. Since this destiny
is union with God in knowledge and love, it is a destiny that must
be freely achieved. Human nature, then, is not a static, ahistorical,
unchangeable structure, but essentially an historical reality: the
history of God's free call and the history of human free response.

In this freedom, then, people stand in the first instance not before God's law, but before God's love:

> The basic meaning of the Christian ethos is not that we must respect objective material norms which God has imposed on reality. For all these material norms become real norms only once they become the expression of the very structure of the person. All other structures of things are placed *below* man. He may alter them, he may twist them as far as he possibly can, he is their master and not their servant. The only ultimate structure of the person which expresses it perfectly is the person's basic capacity for love, and this capacity is boundless.[1]

The capacity to love, created by God's love, is the heart of Christian ethics. According to this ethic, human action is moral when it is in accordance with this basic law or dynamism of human nature, and it is immoral or evil when it goes counter to it.

Scripture speaks often of the primacy of love in Christian life, calling it, for example, the 'first' commandment upon which depends the whole law and the prophets (Matt 22:39–40), and saying that anyone who observes this commandment has fulfilled the whole law (Rom 13:10). But love can be called a 'commandment' or a 'law' only in a sense that is analogous to the other commandments:

> One may speak of a commandment of love as long as one does not forget that this law does not command man to do something or other, but simply commands him to realize himself, and charges man with himself, i.e., himself as the possibility of love in the acceptance of the love in which God does not give something but gives himself.[2]

The primacy of love does not eliminate the importance of the other commandments, for 'there are other values besides love which must not be excluded from the realm of what is moral'.[3]

These other values and the virtues with their specific formal objects are moments within the basic movement and dynamism of love towards the absolute good and ground of all value. Hence it can be said:

Love, which can be experienced only in the movement of an unconditional and trusting surrender of oneself to the unknown, is the real concern of Christian morality, seeing that all the commandments find their ultimate meaning only in love . . .[4]

Such love is the thread which unifies the manifold activities of Christian life and identifies it as Christian: 'If there is love among you, then all will know that you are my disciples' (John 13:35).

It is in this context that Rahner sees the fundamental meaning of human freedom. Freedom in the first instance does not mean the capacity to choose this or that or to do this or that, but the capacity to 'do' and realize oneself. It is the capacity for self-determination, the capacity freely to create one's own identity. Freedom is characterized by the same bipolar structure that characterizes knowledge. Just as in knowledge we are present to ourselves in the process of knowing an object, so too in freedom one is choosing a self in the very process of choosing objective realities: 'The object of freedom in its original sense is the subject himself'.[5]

Freedom never happens as a merely objective exercise, as a mere choice 'between' individual objects, but is the self-realization of the person who chooses objectively; only within this freedom in which man is capable of achieving himself is man also free with regard to the material of his self-achievement.[6]

Hence freedom 'is not the capacity of always being able to do something else, of infinite revision',[7] but the capacity to do something final and definitive, to create a self which is eternal. Freedom as self-realization and self-determination is the 'fundamental option' that is taking place in the course of all one's objective choices.

Freedom in this transcendental sense is an existential of human, spiritual existence. But human beings are not pure spirits. They are also embodied in matter and determined by it, which means that human freedom is finite and limited. It does not create out of whole cloth, but is situated within the confines of limited possibilities, and is exercised 'piecemeal' in space and time over the whole course of a person's life. But this sequence of discrete choices is the gradual enactment and embodiment of one's fundamental option of self-transcending love or its opposite. Hence this fundamental option is not a separate choice by itself, but is the formal object or horizon within which all one's material choices take place. It is the basic orientation that is the motivating force of one's actions. When love is the operative principle of one's life and actions, one can say with Augustine: 'Love, and do what you will'.

It is with this understanding of human nature that Rahner addresses particular questions of natural law. One such question is the ethical legitimacy of contemporary human efforts at 'self-manipulation', which he defines quite simply: 'Self-manipulation means that today man is changing *himself*'.[8] In a sense he has always done this in small ways, but today the possibilities have expanded greatly. A Christian attitude towards this would neither see it with lamentation as a future hell on earth, nor with jubilation as the earthly kingdom of God. It would be at once positive and critical. In his freedom man is *faber sui ipsius*, a being 'who forms and moulds his own nature through culture ... and he may not simply presuppose his nature as a categorical, fixed quantity'.[9] Often in the past, relative and variable elements within human nature have been identified with this nature itself.

Without taking a position on the moral issue involved, Rahner says of the concept of nature employed in the encyclical *Humanae Vitae*:

> It fails to show why the natural constitution of an *individual*, with his particular human powers, *ipso facto* and of itself alone lays a moral demand upon the individual concerned. To say the least the impression it arouses is as though man's capacity deliberately and consciously to shape and direct himself is [a] power added on purely *ab externo* to a closed and 'static' nature, and not that which constitutes human 'nature' precisely as human.[10]

At the same time it must be said that people can act and have acted contrary to their true nature. Efforts at self-manipulation and new forms of social existence, therefore, must not violate the dignity of the individual person nor destroy genuine freedom. Granted this, and not forgetting that it is only through death that one enters the absolute future, openness to change and helping to shape the future is for Christians the medium and historical form of their openness to God's future.

In the light of this, even attempts at 'genetic manipulation' cannot simply be dismissed as unethical, for human beings are 'not simply the product of "nature" ', as though 'nature *alone* were able and authorized to determine and model man's being'.[11] However, some forms of genetic manipulation can certainly be unethical, for example, that involving artificial insemination involving an extra-marital donor. Rahner arrives at this negative moral judgement by what he calls the 'moral instinct of faith, that is, a universal knowledge of right and wrong belief'.[12]

This kind of moral reasoning is necessary wherever complex realities cannot be subjected to an exhaustive analytical reflection, and a judgement is based on more than the logical result of rational considerations. This 'more' is one's moral instinct or sense of what is right and wrong. In this kind of moral knowledge 'what is "objectively" right only becomes transparent to the person who has already embraced the correct attitude to it'.[13] This kind of knowledge is operative in human life in general 'wherever someone is "committed" to a particular attitude'. Such synthesizing knowledge enables one to see the forest in spite of all the trees, and to have the courage to make moral decisions in very complex and ambiguous ethical questions.

The will plays a role in such moral knowledge, and in the instance above one judges that not wanting such genetic manipulation is more Christian and more human than wanting it. This is a legitimate instance where *Stat pro ratione voluntas*, that is, the will supplements purely rational arguments in arriving at a moral judgement. To deny the legitimacy of such moral reasoning in principle is to think that theory always precedes practice in the moral life. Often, however, the opposite is the case:

> Theoretical reflections on norms of practical behaviour emerge from and are necessitated by what has already occurred in practice. But, since it is supposed to be responsible and moral and when it is such, this practice has in itself in principle its own immanent experience of its rectitude.[14]

What is known at this experiential level does not always reach adequate expression on the theoretical level.

There is always the danger, of course, that such prescientific convictions are rooted in historically conditioned prejudices arising out of tradition or society or class ideology. They can then be false and erroneous, and the arguments devised to support them are merely rationalizations. It is always necessary in moral theology, therefore, to examine not only the logical arguments in support of a position, but also the origins of the instinctive convictions that are always operative behind the arguments.[15]

The second aspect of Rahner's systematic theology that has implications for ethics is his notion of the person. From a philosophical point of view and contrary to modern idealism, the individual person is not merely a numerical instance of the species called human nature, but has a unique and positive individuality. Theology, too, affirms that every person has a unique and individual immediacy to the personal and living God. In the light of both philosophy and theology, then, an essential ethics that speaks only of what is incumbent upon every person because of their common essence or nature does not exhaust the responsibility of the individual person in his or her unique situation.

It must be supplemented by an 'existential ethics'.[16] It is called this rather than an individual ethics because it is being contrasted with essential ethics and not social ethics. It must also be distinguished from situation ethics which denies the universal validity of material norms binding on everyone. Existential ethics is not a substitute for such norms, but a supplement to them. From its perspective sin is not just a violation of these general norms, but also a personal failure of love.

To answer the difficult question of how one comes to know such an existential demand of conscience, Rahner turns to the method developed by Ignatius Loyola for discovering God's will for an individual.[17] Since such knowledge cannot be deduced from general principles, it must be 'in some sense directly due to God himself'. At the same time it must be distinguished from revelation in the proper sense, since it is not an exceptional phenomenon in Christian life.[18] He concludes that it is derived from a non-conceptual experience of God wherein that transcendence to God which accompanies all knowledge emerges into the forefront of awareness, and the usual conceptual object recedes into the background, becomes 'more transparent' and 'can almost entirely disappear'.[19] One has thereby a sense of immediacy with and is in touch with God himself, not a concept of him, so that the 'consolation' involved has no cause or object other than God himself. According to the Ignatian rules for the discernment of spirits, when the object of one's proposed choice or 'election' is found to be in harmony with this consolation, giving rise to 'peace and tranquillity', one has discovered God's will for oneself in this experiential way.

Finally, Rahner's understanding of the relationship between God and the world has implications for moral theology. We do not encounter God in knowledge and love as one object among others in the world:

> God is not an object towards which the intentionality of man can be directed in the same fragmentary and particular way as it is towards the multiplicity of objects and persons encountered within the categories of intramundane experience ... In the original act which precedes all reflective systematisations, God is always given as the subjectively and objectively all-bearing *ground* of experience, a ground which is beyond this world.[20]

In human transcendence elevated by grace, God is present and experienced indirectly and implicitly in every act directed towards the world, and pre-eminently in the act of self-transcending love.

In the moral choice to love one's neighbour God is also chosen and loved in the very choice to love. For in becoming one with one's neighbour in love, one is also becoming one with God who is love. God is experienced and loved in this relationship not as its thematic, material object, which is precisely one's neighbour, but as the formal object and horizon of the relationship. In the words of John, when one keeps the commandment of love, one 'dwells' in God's love (John 15:10), or one 'is born of God and knows God' (1 John 4:8).

The theological virtues of faith and love by which we are able to know and love God are mediated by our relationship to the world. This primary, unthematic experience of God can, of course, be objectified into a concept of God which can become the explicit object of knowledge and love. But the object of this religious act is secondary and derivative, and the act itself is once again borne by the unthematic experience of which it speaks. One can say that measured by its object the religious act is of a higher dignity than an act dealing with a finite object. But:

> Measured by its 'horizon' or its transcendental possibility, it has the same dignity, the same 'draught' and the same radicality as the act of explicit love of neighbour, since both acts are necessarily supported by the (experienced but unreflected) reference both to God and to the intramundane Thou and this by grace (of infused *caritas*), i.e., by that on which the explicit acts both

of our relationship to God and of our love of neighbour 'for God's sake' reflect.[21]

Love for one's neighbour, then, is not 'a secondary moral act' required by love of God, but rather 'love of neighbour is the primary act of the love of God'.[22]

This single act of love which embraces both God and neighbour 'allows the eternal kingdom of God to begin' and 'is the miracle of the birth of eternity'.[23] These statements express the hope which is an integral part of love and reveal Rahner's basic approach to hope and eschatology. The eternal kingdom of God which is the object of the theological virtue of hope is best conceived not as coming 'after' time in a kind of temporal succession, but as coming to be within time as the fruit of freedom and love. Hope in God's future has the same structure as love for God, namely, its thematic, material object is an intramundane future which is both borne by and mediates hope in the absolute future.[24]

Eschatological statements in Scripture and Tradition, therefore, must be interpreted not as giving us an eyewitness description of this absolute future, but as expressing 'the futurity of the present'.[25] It is on this basis that Rahner distinguishes eschatology from apocalyptic:

> Biblical eschatology must always be read as an assertion based on the revealed present and pointing towards the genuine future, but not as an assertion pointing back from an anticipated future into the present. To extrapolate from the present into the future is eschatology, to interpolate from the future into the present is apocalyptic.[26]

Rahner sees the latter as 'either phantasy or gnosticism', devaluing history as the real ground from which eternity emerges.

To express the relationship between history and the eschaton Rahner speaks of the latter as the 'consummation' of history. The notion of consummation implies that an historical event not only has an end in the sense that it ceases, but also that it produces a result, 'something definitive which is different from the event itself'. This result produced in time, moreover, is that for which the event considered in its temporal development took place, 'that which it "sought" and in which the event itself finds its meaning and its justification'.[27] Such a consummation would be 'immanent' if the result is produced by resources proper to its own being and its own intrinsic tendency, and would be transcendent if it were conferred *ab externo* and independently of the agent's own actions.

In the case of the history of human freedom wherein God's Spirit is its innermost dynamism, its immanent consummation *is* its transcendent consummation and vice versa. For 'the transcendent consummation of a personal freedom is the only true immanent consummation'.[28] The eschaton is the consummation of the history of an individual person and of the collective history of humankind as a whole. Moreover, given the intrinsic relationship between matter and spirit, the material world and the whole process of history are not cast aside or left behind at the end of history, but share in this final consummation.[29]

We must speak of the eschatological consummation of history in both an individual and a collective sense because the human person is both an individual and a social being. As unique individuals we are endowed with freedom and responsibility for our own destiny, and as members of the larger history of the human race our individual destiny is related to the destiny of all. This collective history is not merely the place where individual dramas are played out on the stage of the world, but 'the *whole* is a drama, and the stage itself is also part of it'.[30] For the history of God's offer of salvation and the individual's free acceptance of it does not take place alongside the history of the world, but within it as its innermost meaning. Whatever can be achieved, then, in the realization of inner-worldly hopes and the transformation of the present world is part of history's movement towards God's kingdom. Between these hopes and eschatological hope stands a relationship of 'unity and difference',[31] not an identity, for the path to eternity passes through the portal of death.

Death represents the first element treated in the traditional eschatology of the individual person, and Rahner develops this treatment from several points of view in his theology of death. A human being can be considered both as nature and as person, and death can be understood from both of these aspects.[32] As a natural event, death is a necessary fact of life, something which happens to everyone. It is part of being human and something which everyone must suffer and accept. But as persons human beings are free and self-determining, and from this aspect death is a deed, something which every person must do and do freely.

In its natural aspect death is understood as the definitive end of one's earthly pilgrimage, and is described as the 'separation of body and soul'. This description is often taken to mean that the soul leaves the world and becomes 'acosmic':

> This conception prevails because by instinct—or, to speak more precisely, under the persistent influence of a Neoplatonic mentality—we tend to assume that the appearance of the soul before God, which, faith teaches us, takes place at death, stands in some direct opposition to her present relationship to the world, as though freedom from matter and nearness to God must increase by a direct ratio.[33]

Given the fact that the soul through the body has a relationship to the whole of the material universe in its unity, Rahner prefers to think of the soul at death not as becoming acosmic, but as entering into a new relationship to the world as a whole in its unity. He calls this relationship 'pancosmic', not in the sense that the soul informs the world or is omnipresent, but in the sense that it is open to and related to the totality of the universe in its unity.[34]

This description of death as the separation of body and soul does not express the specifically human and personal aspect of death as an event of the whole person, and indeed happening throughout the whole of life. Human existence is a 'being unto death' all through life, and this 'existential' co-determines everything in life and imparts to it its ultimate seriousness. Death gives freedom its 'once and for all' character. Every act of letting go of the self in surrender to the mystery of God in faith and hope, every act of self-transcendence in love for God and neighbour is part of the process of dying. Such Christian dying takes place throughout all of life in various degrees of intensity. From this aspect dying is a deed in freedom and constitutes the fundamental option of Christian living: to lose self in order to find one's true self. This self-disposal and self-determination in freedom need not, and usually does not, take place in the last hours of life or at the moment of clinical death. Rather in what Gregory the Great calls the *prolixitas mortis*, freedom inescapably confronts death in acceptance or protest throughout the whole of life.[35]

Examples of this *prolixitas mortis* are numerous and varied. There is the ongoing experience of the transitoriness and perishability of all the realities of life and of one's own finiteness in the face of this. All human experiences of suffering, disappointment or failure are heralds and intimations of mortality. The ongoing infiltration of death into life and the vulnerability of life are felt most keenly in the face of serious and life-threatening illness which affects not just the body but the whole self. Nor can the courage to keep a 'stiff upper lip' nor any amount of maturity and 'growing up' render a person immune to the radical threat in these experiences. They remain challenges to freedom to accept this human condition in faith and hope, or to protest in anger, or resign oneself in despair.

The necessity and universality of death have been seen in Christian tradition as the penalty of sin, as the 'wages of sin'. Rahner interprets this to mean not that death in a biological sense, as the natural end of all living things, or in an anthropological sense, as the end of a person's history of freedom, would not occur had there been no sin. Rather, it is the concrete mode in which we experience death and dying that is the consequence of sin. He characterizes this mode as the 'hiddenness of death' or the 'darkness of death'.[36] The history of a person's freedom as self-determination stands in a dialectical relationship to the fact that one is utterly at God's disposal, a fact which becomes fully realized and fully manifest in death:

> Only in the dialectic between freedom and disposability, completely radicalized in death and in such a way that the concreteness of this dialectic is still absolutely hidden from man, is the real nature of 'infralapsarian' death present that makes it possible for death in this hidden dialectic (beyond our understanding) to be the manifestation of sin and redemption and liberation.[37]

Because of sin and concupiscence, which Rahner understands as the inability to integrate all the plural elements of human existence into the free and basic option of openness to the mystery of God, no one is able to die 'in integrity' in this sense, or to know the outcome of the hidden dialectic of freedom. Hence there is justified pain and fear in the face of the darkness of death which ought not to be and would not be, had human history been only a history of grace.

Rahner considers this situation to be due both to original sin and to personal sin, though the term 'sin' is applied to both only in an analogous sense. To understand the nature of original sin he emphasizes that sin at the origin or beginning of human history, whether this is understood as the sin of a single person (monogenism) or of a group (polygenism), happens at the beginning not just in the sense of the first of a whole series of moments, but in the sense of the basis upon which this whole history rests. Sin at the beginning in this sense thwarted the intention of God that descent from this origin was to have been the medium 'in which that justifying holiness of man was communicated to him which is prior to his own personal existence, and therefore has the force of an existential modality':

> The absence of that holiness which is an existential modality imparted by God's own holiness prior to the concrete conditions of individual existence, inasmuch as this was intended to be mediated through human descent but in fact is not so—this is rightly called a state of sinfulness, and it is this that is meant by original sin (*peccatum originale originatum*).[38]

This universal state of sinfulness stands in dialectical relationship to God's universal saving will which imparts to everyone through Christ, at least as an offer, that sanctification which was not imparted through descent from Adam. As realities prior to a person's free decision, both original sin and redemptive grace in their dialectical relationship determine the situation into which everyone is born.

In this understanding, original sin has nothing to do with the notion of 'collective guilt', nor with the imputation of the guilt of Adam to his descendants, nor with the transmission of this guilt to successive generations biologically or otherwise. Everyone's relationship to God is determined by the exercise of their own freedom. But this exercise of freedom always takes place in a situation that is determined by history and by other persons, and in the light of original sin, this means determined by sin and evil. Though it is the situation and realm of freedom that is so determined and not freedom itself, this does not mean that the situation is purely external to freedom:

> It is not the external material in which an intention, an attitude or a decision is merely actualized in such a way that the material of this free decision then drops off this decision, as it were. Rather freedom inevitably appropriates the material in which it actualizes itself as an intrinsic and constitutive element . . .[39]

A simple example which Rahner gives to illustrate how a sinful situation can enter into one's free decision is the purchase of bananas at a price based on a commercial policy that is unjust towards those involved in picking bananas. Wittingly or unwittingly, one's purchase contributes to maintaining the situation and its social injustice.

Though Scripture ascribes death in the concrete form of pain and darkness in which we experience it to original and personal sin, it also speaks of death from the perspective of grace as 'dying with Christ' (Rom 6:8). Because his death is the paradigm for all Christian dying, we must keep in mind in what sense his death was redemptive and liberating:

> ... this redemption came about by the very fact that death as manifestation of sin, as the visibility of the emptiness and hopelessness of this sin, as domain of eternal darkness and God-forsakenness, was accepted in faith, hope and love, and transformed in the midst of desolation and loneliness into the manifestation of the obedient surrender of the whole person to the incomprehensibility of the holy God.[40]

Just as the death of Jesus was the culmination of his life, so too Christian dying is the culmination of the life of grace which conforms our life to his. In the total powerlessness and vulnerability of death the renunciation, surrender and loss of self which are the heart of all believing, hoping and loving become radical and final. Christian dying as a free act of faith, hope and love transforms the manifestation of sin into a manifestation of grace.

Such a death is passage into eternal life. It follows from Rahner's interpretation of eschatological statements that we cannot imagine or conceive what the final and eternal consummation of the world and of individual and collective history will be like, as Paul stressed when asked about the nature of a risen body (1 Cor 15:35–46). The image of eternity that most readily and almost inevitably suggests itself is that of an endless continuation of time after death. But eternity 'does not mean that things continue on after death as though, as Feuerbach put it, we only change horses and then ride on'.[41] Rather, eternal life 'comes to be in time as time's own mature fruit', and 'comes to be *through* death, not *after* it'. This coming to be of one's eternal life takes place wherever there is dying to self in the life of grace, which is precisely participation in God's eternal life, and this process becomes final through death.

Eternity, then, must be understood not as a mode of time, but from a correct understanding of the life of the spirit in freedom.[42] Rahner suggests three areas where our experience in time is also an experience of something more than time as a succession of moments coming to be and passing away. First, we experience the permanence of a reality enduring through successive changes in time and express this in the term 'substance'. Secondly, there is the mind's ability to gather past, present and future together and thus to shape and unify time. Finally and most importantly, we experience in free decisions which accept moral responsibility in absolute fidelity to conscience something that has a finality that does not pass away. 'Here time really creates eternity and eternity is experienced in time.'[43] When Scripture speaks, then, of eternal union with God in various images as rest and peace, as glory, as a heavenly banquet, or as the community of the blessed in their Father's house, they all point to that life with God which is not bestowed merely as an external reward from without, but is the very life and the very self one has created through time in grace and freedom.

Christian tradition also speaks of an 'intermediate state' between death and the resurrection of the body. Given the difficulties involved in conceiving of the soul 'separated' from the body, Rahner prefers to think that the single and total perfecting of a person in 'body' and 'soul' takes place immediately in and through death.[44] One can maintain this because the identity of the glorified body with the earthly body cannot consist in an identity of physical matter. For such an identity cannot be found even in the earthly body because of the ongoing process of metabolic change. Hence resurrection can be thought to coincide with 'that particular moment when the person's history of freedom is finally consummated, which is to say at . . . death'.[45]

Associated with the intermediate state is the doctrine of purgatory, a place or state of purification after death. If at death the many levels of one's total reality have not been integrated into a basic option for God, it makes sense to speak of an interim period where this final maturing process takes place. It labours, however, under the obvious difficulties of having to think of purgatory in temporal categories 'after death' even though it is beyond time.[46] To avoid this difficulty, Rahner asks whether the notion of purgatory can be brought into closer proximity with the pain and darkness of death and the whole process of dying in its many phases.[47] Or can purgatory be seen in the light of a modified theory of the 'transmigration of souls', which might also be useful in cases such as those of infants who die without the opportunity of freely choosing God?[48] In any case, distinguishing between the content of the doctrines both of an intermediate state and of purgatory, and the conceptual model in which they are understood, opens up the possibility of understanding them in other ways.

Christian eschatology includes the possibility of an opposite judgement at the end of an individual's history of freedom, that of eternal damnation called hell. Judgement is understood not as a purely extrinsic 'sentence', but as the intrinsic consequence of a person's fundamental option against God. Hell must be a possibility, for otherwise the history of freedom loses its seriousness and the radical difference between good and evil is annulled.[49] But the doctrines of heaven and hell are not parallel:

What Christianity really proclaims as essential is not the equal possibility of these *two* ways of passing from time to eternity, but the victory of the love of God who bestows himself in and through our freedom: it points to the cross and resurrection of Jesus as to the event of this now manifest victory of God's love.[50]

Statements in the New Testament about eternal loss can be interpreted as asserting this as a possibility for every individual, not as affirming its actuality. Indeed, Christians must hope that in the end God's grace will ultimately triumph over every evil. For Christianity is essentially a message of faith and hope in the power of God's love.

Notes

1   'The "commandment" of love in relation to the other commandments', TI 5, p. 456.

2   Ibid.

3   Ibid., p. 439.

4   Ibid., p. 454.

5   FC, p. 38.

6   'Theology of freedom', TI 6, p. 185.

7   Ibid., p. 186.

8   'The experiment with man: theological observations on man's self-manipulation', TI 9, p. 206.

9   Ibid., p. 216.

10   'On the encyclical "Humanae Vitae" ', TI 11, p. 277.

11   'The problem of genetic manipulation' TI 9, p. 227.

12 Ibid., p. 238.

13 Ibid.

14 'On bad arguments in moral theology', TI 18, p. 75.

15 Ibid., p. 78.

16 'On the question of a formal existential ethics', TI 2, pp. 217–34.

17 'The logic of concrete individual knowledge in Ignatius Loyola', *The Dynamic Element in the Church* (*Quaestiones Disputatae* 12; New York: Herder & Herder/London: Burns & Oates, 1964), pp. 84–170.

18 Ibid., p. 106.

19 Ibid., pp. 145–50.

20 'Reflections on the unity of the love of neighbour and the love of God', TI 6, p. 244.

21 Ibid., p. 246.

22 Ibid., p. 247.

23 Ibid., p. 231.

24 'On the theology of hope', TI 10, pp. 256–9.

25 'The hermeneutics of eschatological assertions', TI 4, p. 332.

26 Ibid., p. 337.

27 'Immanent and transcendent consummation of the world', TI 10, pp. 274–5.

28 Ibid., p. 279.

29 Ibid., pp. 284–9.

30 FC, p. 446.

31 Ibid., p. 447.

32 *On the Theology of Death* (*Quaestiones Disputatae* 2; Freiburg: Herder/London: Nelson, 1961/New York: Herder & Herder, 1962), p. 21.

33 Ibid., pp. 27–8.

34 Ibid., pp. 26–31.

35 'Christian dying', TI 18, pp. 228–30.

36 Ibid., pp. 247–52.

37 Ibid., p. 244.

38 'The sin of Adam', TI 11, p. 256.

39 FC, p. 107.

40 'Christian dying', p. 253.

41 FC, p. 436.

42 'The life of the dead', TI 4, p. 348.

43 'Eternity from time', TI 19, p. 175.

44 ' "The intermediate state" ', TI 17, p. 115.

45 Ibid., p. 120.

46 FC, pp. 441–2.

47 'Purgatory', TI 19, pp. 185–7.

48 Ibid., pp. 192–3.

49 FC, pp. 443–4.

50 'Eternity from time', p. 177.

10

The Trinity

The Trinity, which is the most comprehensive doctrine elaborated in the Christian tradition to express all the elements of the experience of God in salvation history, is also the common thread which unifies all the various elements in Rahner's theology. Every theological topic is an aspect of this central mystery, so that 'the doctrine of God is not complete until the end of the last dogmatic treatise'.[1] But even then it is complete only in a very relative sense:

> We are rightly always engaged in *systematising* . . . but we never *have* a system; we always know more than what we have already systematised, and this unsystematised extra in our fundamentally plural experience is not merely supplementary to what we have mastered by system, but constitutes an incommensurate challenge and threat to it, and is its future corrective.[2]

Theology's task is always unfinished because its single topic is the inexhaustible mystery of the trinitarian God. Rahner finds this emphasis on the centrality of the Trinity especially exemplified in the Greek Fathers for whom 'the *whole* of their theology was a treatise on the Trinity'.[3]

Christian faith, then, is about 'the one mystery with which the Christian revelation confronts mankind'.[4] We can miss the forest for the trees, however, because we speak of the many 'mysteries' of faith as though God could have revealed more or other mysteries, and we think of mystery primarily in a negative sense as the property of a statement we cannot understand. We also assume these truths are only provisionally mysterious until they are rendered comprehensible in the beatific vision.[5] But, prior to propositions *about* God, faith confronts the very reality of God himself who is present in his self-revelation and self-communication. This reality of 'God with us' is *the* mystery of Christian faith, and this mystery in its positive sense is not only provisional, for seeing God face to face in the beatific vision is seeing and accepting God as forever mystery. In the concrete order of salvation the mystery of God with us is the mystery of his presence as Logos in the Incarnation and as Spirit in divinizing grace, and these together are the three facets of the single mystery of the Trinity.[6]

It is clear that Rahner is speaking here of the mystery of the Trinity in salvation history as God with us and for us, and it could be thought that this opens up the way to the further mystery of God as he is in himself, or the mystery of the immanent Trinity. The former could be thought to be the jumping-off point for speculation about the still profounder mystery of God's own inner-trinitarian life. But because of the nature of the Incarnation and the nature of grace, Rahner rejects this move:

> God has given himself so fully in his absolute self-communication to the creature, that the 'immanent' Trinity becomes the Trinity of the 'economy of salvation', and hence in turn the Trinity of salvation which we experience *is* the immanent Trinity. This means that the Trinity of God's relationship to us *is* the reality of God as he is *in* himself: a trinity of persons.[7]

Hence 'there is no real difference' between 'God in himself' and 'God for us' because 'At least since Christ and in him we are both obliged and empowered to be continually overstepping this distinction'.[8] For to be with us just as he is in himself is exactly what he desires. Rahner reflects both on the nature of the Incarnation and on the nature of grace to arrive at his fundamental axiom of the identity of the immanent Trinity with the Trinity in salvation history.

The Incarnation provides one instance and one point at which this fundamental axiom is incontrovertible, for the Logos actually *became* man in Jesus. Hence the immanent Logos of the eternal, inner-trinitarian life and the Logos in salvation history are strictly identical. Moreover, Rahner maintains that only the Logos among the divine persons could have become incarnate. For if this were not the case:

> There would be no longer any real and intrinsic connection between the mission of a divine person and the immanent life of the Trinity. Our sonship in grace would have absolutely nothing to do with the sonship of the Son, since it would have been absolutely the same if it could have been based on any other incarnate person of the Godhead. There would be no way of finding out, from what God is to us, what he is in himself as the Trinity.[9]

The role of the Logos in salvation history as the Word and expression of God follows from and reveals his eternal reality as the inner-trinitarian expression of the Father. It is false to assume that because the Logos became man any one of the other divine hypostases or persons could also have done so, because it is precisely as hypostasis or person that the three are different and distinct. The term 'hypostasis' when applied to the Trinity is not a univocal concept with only one meaning and application, but refers in a unique way to each of the three.

A further consideration strengthens still more the identity of the immanent and economic Logos. Are we to assume that the human nature assumed by the Logos is an alien element, something already given antecedently and having nothing intrinsic to do with the Logos, or is it precisely that which comes to be when the Logos is expressed into what is not divine? Is human nature already known independently of the Incarnation, or is it to be ultimately explained on the basis of the self-emptying self-expression of the Logos? In the former case it could be said formally that the Logos was present and active in the world by means of this human nature, but the latter as such would reveal nothing of the Logos. At most he would display through this human nature miraculous and superhuman features, preternatural traits which belong to no other human nature. But the human as such would not reveal the Logos as such.[10]

But the relationship between the Logos and the human nature assumed in Christ is more essential and intrinsic:

> Human nature in general is a possible object of the creative knowledge and power of God, because and in so far as the Word is essentially the expressible, he who can be expressed even in the non-divine, being the Word of the Father, in whom the Father

can express himself and—freely—exteriorise himself, and because, when this takes place, that which we call human nature comes into being.[11]

The human nature is not a mask assumed from without which hides the Logos while he acts things out in the world, but from the start is the constitutive and real symbol of the Logos himself. We can and must say, then, that in his deepest ontological origin 'man is possible because the exteriorisation of the Logos is possible'.[12] Not just what Jesus says, but what he is and does as man *is* and reveals the Logos himself as our salvation among us. In this instance, then, the Logos with God and the Logos with us, the immanent and the economic Logos, are one and the same.

To show that this is indeed an instance and a paradigm for understanding the entire Trinity, Rahner turns to the doctrine of grace. In the life of grace each of the divine persons has a proper, not just appropriated, relationship to the justified person, and this means:

> Each one of the three divine persons communicates himself to man in gratuitous grace in his own personal particularity and diversity. This trinitarian communication is the ontological ground of man's life of grace and eventually of the direct vision of the divine persons in eternity. It is God's 'indwelling', 'uncreated grace', understood not only as a communication of the divine nature, but also and primarily, since it implies a free personal act, since it occurs from person to person, as a communication of 'persons'.[13]

This one divine self-communication of the persons occurs according to their mutual relations, that is, according to the three relative ways in which God subsists, so that their threefold relationship to us expresses outwards their own inner-trinitarian relations. This single yet threefold relationship to us is not just an image or analogy of the Trinity, but the triune personal God himself as freely bestowed in uncreated grace. Since each of the three divine persons has not just an appropriated relationship to us, which would tell us nothing about the Trinity, but a proper relationship, the Trinity experienced in the history of salvation *is* the triune God as he is in himself.

Rahner then looks at grace from the other direction to arrive at the same conclusion. He points out that grace is an actual *self*-communication of God to us. We are related to God in grace not indirectly through some finite reality which he produces by efficient causality, and to which he remains extrinsic as its efficient cause. Rather in grace he bestows *himself* directly in a relationship that comes about through what can best be called quasi-formal causality.[14] Calling it such expresses the fact that in grace God is not just the giver, but the gift as well. Now Scripture gives witness to the threefold aspect of the gift of God's presence when it speaks of the Father sending both the Son and the Spirit. These are not just three words for the same thing, but point to a real distinction in the manner of God's presence in salvation history. If this threefold presence is a genuine *self*-communication of God, then this threefoldness must also be true of God as he is in himself.

To maintain otherwise would be to deny that grace is a real self-communication of God. Moreover, maintaining that grace is such a communication precludes an Arian interpretation of grace, in which God's presence would only be mediated by created realities. It also precludes a modalistic or Sabellian interpretation, wherein the modes of God's presence to us tell us nothing about the reality of God. From this vantage point too, then, the Trinity experienced in salvation history *is* the immanent Trinity of God's own life.[15]

If one accepts this basic axiom of the identity of the immanent and economic Trinity, the doctrine of the Trinity is seen in an entirely new light. The heart of the doctrine is no longer an abstruse and esoteric theory about the nature of God, concerned mainly with the logical compatibility of God being both one and three, but is the mystery of salvation itself, the mystery of God with us. Revelation gives us not just an abstract doctrine about the Trinity, but bestows on us the very reality about which the doctrine speaks. If the doctrine of the Trinity did not concern our salvation, says Rahner, it would not have been revealed. Hence we may 'confidently look for an access into the doctrine of the Trinity in Jesus and in his Spirit, as we experience them through faith in salvation history'.[16] Awareness that our real knowledge of God comes through the experience of Jesus and his Spirit in salvation history protects us 'against the danger of tacitly making an abstract metaphysical schema into the *norma non normata* of what, how and who God "can be" '.[17]

As a typical example of this danger, Rahner mentions the 'undialectical idea of God's "immutability" ' functioning as the norm for understanding the scriptural assertion that 'the Word became flesh', rather than Scripture itself being the norm for our understanding of God.[18] Such an approach would also give paramount importance not to God's 'metaphysically necessary attributes', but to his 'freely adopted disposition towards man and the world' as revealed in his action in salvation history:

> His faithfulness, mercy, love, in short the concrete relationship of God to us ... are not merely the theologically attested necessary 'attributes' of God's metaphysical being, but considerably more. For God could deny us the very faithfulness, love etc. which he actually shows towards us, without ceasing to be faithful and loving in a metaphysical sense. And to recognise this possibility, to confide in the marvel of the *free* love of God, is to open up the horizon within which his attributes can really be grasped as being *divine*, i.e., such that a knowledge of them does not give us any power over him.[19]

Rahner sees here a possible rapprochement between the Catholic approach to the knowledge of God and the Lutheran emphasis on the *theologia crucis*, that is, Luther's doctrine that our knowledge of God must be drawn from the crucified Jesus in his humiliation, not from the use of human reason.

When the immanent Trinity is seen as identical with the economic Trinity, the focus of systematic theology shifts to the economic Trinity itself. Beginning with the scriptural testimony that the self-communication of God, understood in the scriptural sense as God the Father, takes place in two ways, through the sending of both the Son and the Spirit, the question it asks is this:

> How can these two ways be understood as moments, innerly related to each other, yet distinct from one another, of the *one* self-communication of God, in such a way that the distinction too may really be brought under a 'concept'?[20]

The two moments themselves of the mission of the Son and the Spirit are developed fully in Christology and the theology of the Spirit. The task of trinitarian theology is to throw light on their intrinsic and mutual interrelationship. Granted that God's self-communication is free, theology asks what it is about the nature of this communication that requires that it take place in the two ways attested to in Scripture. This is not an attempt to deduce the two ways, but rather, beginning with the scriptural facts, to ask why it must be the Son who appears historically in the flesh as man, and why it must be the Spirit who brings about the acceptance of this self-communication.

Rahner suggests four aspects, not necessarily the only ones, under which the two moments of God's self-communication can be paired so as to throw light on their necessary unity and difference. The first element of each pair refers to the Son and the second to the Spirit: '(a) Origin–Future; (b) History–Transcendence; (c) Invitation–Acceptance; (d) Knowledge–Love'.[21] Each one of these pairs follows from the fact that God's self-communication is free and is addressed to an historical and free being.

To counter the possible objection that the necessity of this duality is based on the nature of man who receives God's communication, and tells us nothing about God who is doing the communicating, it must be remembered that the creation of human nature took place in view of and for the sake of this self-communication, that it is the condition which makes possible the existence of an addressee. If, then, God's self-communication is to be freely offered and freely accepted in a genuine personal relationship, it must include the sending of both the Son and the Spirit in their different roles.

The first aspect mentioned above to clarify these roles is origin–future: The origin or creation of all things in and through the Logos for the sake of God's self-communication is distinguished by a real history of freedom from the future realization of this purpose in and through the power of the Spirit. Secondly, history–transcendence: The realization of this purpose freely in history, most especially in the Incarnation of the Logos, is distinguished from the transcendence of history towards the absolute future of God through the dynamism of the Spirit. Thirdly, invitation–acceptance: This realization includes both the offer or invitation revealed through the Son and its acceptance through the power of the Spirit. Finally, knowledge–love: This revelation in the Son gives us knowledge of the truth of both God and ourselves, the truth of God's love for us, and this truth elicits and begets our own free response of love, that love which is the very Spirit dwelling within us and 'enabling us to cry Abba! Father!' (Rom 8:15).[22] Thus each aspect clarifies from its own vantage point the mutual interdependence of the Son and the Spirit in the process of the Father's self-communication.

Rahner's next step is to show that each side of these four pairs constitutes a unity, so that there are two and only two basic modalities or missions in God's self-communication. Looking at the first side, namely, origin, history, invitation, truth, one can say that all creation has its origin in God's free self-utterance outwards in the

Logos, and its history is the coming to be of the humanity which can receive the invitation of God's self-communication, a process which reaches the 'fullness of time' and is revealed in the fullness of its irrevocable truth in the Incarnation of the Logos. Looking at the second side, namely, future, transcendence, acceptance, love, one can say that it is the power of the Spirit whose love begets love which brings about the free acceptance of this invitation in an openness and transcendence towards the consummation of history in the absolute future of God.

Summing up the four elements of each side into a 'short formula', Rahner names the two basic modalities of God's self-communication as 'history' and 'spirit':

> The divine self-communication occurs in unity and distinction in history (of the truth) and in the spirit (of love).[23]

Seeing in this way the necessary and interrelated roles of the Son and the Spirit shows that God in salvation history not only is Trinity, as Scripture tells us, but must be.

This 'must', moreover, has implications beyond God's free presence and activity in history. If this presence and activity is the process of God's self-communication, then the triune differentiation within God in salvation history must be true of God as he is 'in himself'. The economic Trinity must be the immanent Trinity and vice versa. Indeed, the latter is the condition which makes the former possible:

> There is real difference in God as he is in himself between one and the same God insofar as he is—at once and necessarily—the unoriginate who mediates himself to himself (Father), the one who is truth uttered for himself (Son), and the one who is received and accepted in love for himself (Spirit)—and insofar as, *as a result of this*, he is the one who can freely communicate himself.[24]

Because God is truth and love in himself, he can share this same truth and love in his self-communication to what is not divine. Moreover, because this Trinity is constituted by real and distinct relations of truth and love within *one* God, 'the doctrine of the Trinity can and must be understood not as a supplement or an attenuation of Christian monotheism, but as its radicalization . . .'.[25]

In this light it is not accidental that in speaking of the Trinity

Rahner avoids the term 'persons' to express the relations within God. He points out that the term does not mean today what it meant when it was applied to the Trinity. When we use the term in the plural today we almost inevitably think of distinct and separate subjectivities, that is, several conscious and free centres of activity. To think of God as 'three persons' in this sense is to think of a tritheism of three Gods rather than the Trinity. For God is a single centre of consciousness, freedom and activity, shared in by Father, Son and Spirit each in a unique way. The term 'three persons', moreover, attempts to generalize and add up what cannot be added up, for Father, Son and Spirit are unique in what distinguishes them from each other. The threeness in God does not constitute a 'group-building multiplication'. It can also be said that this term was not used from the beginning by the New Testament or the early Fathers to express their knowledge in faith of the Father, Son and Spirit, so that it cannot be said to be *absolutely* constitutive of this knowledge.[26]

Nevertheless, the Church has a right to regulate the language in which its confession of faith is expressed, and 'three persons' in God has in fact become the language of the Church. One can, however, try to devise a concept, not to replace, but to explain what 'person' means, and thus to avoid the misunderstandings mentioned above. Rahner suggests the following formulation: 'The one God subsists in three distinct manners of subsisting'.[27] In the explanatory concept 'distinct manner of subsisting', the term 'subsisting' is meant to emphasize the irreducible distinctness and uniqueness of the Father, Son and Spirit in their relational reality. The term 'manner' is meant to suggest their unity, that it is one God who subsists in these ways.

To speak of 'three' manners, of course, labours under the same difficulty mentioned above about adding what cannot be added. Hence it is necessary to stress that 'manner of subsisting' is an analogous concept that is applied to Father, Son and Spirit in a way that is unique and proper to each of them. In spite of the highly formal and abstract nature of the concept, it can function as an explanatory corrective to misunderstandings of the term 'person'.

Rahner's whole approach to the Trinity differs considerably from the traditional use, going all the way back to Augustine, of a 'psychological analogy' to clarify the oneness and threeness of God. While acknowledging that the two basic activities of the human spirit, knowledge and love, justifiably recommend themselves as an analogy for understanding the two processions of the Logos and

Spirit in God, he raises two basic problems about this psychological speculation and its 'strangely isolated individualism'. First, the analogy does not really explain what it is meant to explain, namely, why divine knowledge and love necessarily require the processions of Word and Spirit as distinct manners of subsisting, or, in the more traditional terminology, as distinct 'persons'. Secondly, in developing its speculations about the immanent Trinity it leaves behind and forgets the real and only source of our knowledge of the Trinity, namely, its presence to us in salvation history. If we stay in touch with this source, and realize that in the experience of the two ways of God's self-communication to us as truth and as love the two processions of the immanent Trinity are already co-known, we would have in this experience a more fruitful basis for a psychological understanding of the Trinity.[28]

In saying this, Rahner is not merely recommending that the immanent and the economic Trinity be brought more closely together, as though they each had a prior existence as two separate realities. Rather, he is insisting once again on their prior unity and identity. To grasp this is to avoid the false notion 'that a "pure" dogma of the immanent Trinity can evolve which is totally different from the doctrine of the economic Trinity'.[29] The notion is false because revelation is the presence of the very reality of the Trinity itself, not the communication of an idea about it. God as he is in himself is present in our individual and collective history, 'bidding us enter in (ultimately into the love of one's neighbour)'.[30] Here lies the source of our one knowledge of the Trinity. In his theology of grace Rahner insists that 'pure human nature' is only an abstract possibility, outstripped by God's self-communication in grace. Perhaps the parallel in his doctrine of God would be to say that 'pure divine nature' and a 'pure doctrine of the immanent Trinity' are also but abstract possibilities, outstripped by God's sovereign freedom in becoming man.

In the actual order in which we exist, then, the Trinity is not just our most comprehensive doctrine of God, but also our most comprehensive doctrine of God and the world. It is for this reason that Rahner points with regret to the fact that it seems to have become a 'forgotten truth' in the religious life of Christians. In spite of our orthodox profession of faith, for all practical purposes we have become 'almost mere monotheists', and should the doctrine of the Trinity be dropped, 'the major part of religious literature could well remain virtually unchanged'.[31] To see the importance of the doctrine of the Trinity in shaping religious life and the religious imagination one need only reflect on the truncated version of Christian faith that results from forgetting any one of its three elements: the Father as utterly transcendent to the world, the Son as incarnate and present in history, and the Spirit as immanent within the world as its inner-most dynamism.

Focusing on God only as purely transcendent and forgetting the sending of the Son and the Spirit, a 'mere monotheism' in this sense, would result in a form of deism, a notion of God who is sequestered in heaven and separated from us who dwell on earth. Focusing only on the immanence of God and forgetting his transcendence leads to the opposite of deism, a pantheism that simply identifies God with the world and the world with God. Focusing only on the Son and history leads to 'pure humanism', a 'secular interpretation of the Gospel' that pretends to be its exhaustive interpretation. A religion exclusively of the 'Spirit', on the other hand, is a religion of pure interiority, a form of pietism or quietism or disembodied religiosity that is indifferent to history. Each element is a partial truth which becomes false when it is made the whole truth. The doctrine of the Trinity is meant to include all of these elements in their dialectical relationships, and to speak of God and the world as never identical, but also never separate.

In his understanding of the Trinity Rahner also emphasizes the unity of God to avoid the opposite extreme to monotheism, that of tritheism. He alluded to this in his discussion of the danger of separating God into 'three persons' in the modern sense. Perhaps a symptom of this danger can be seen in the tension found in places in the Second Vatican Council's Pastoral Constitution on the Church in the Modern World. While affirming that 'the love of God cannot be separated from the love of neighbour' (no. 24), and that our eschatological hope in a new earth must not be separated from inner-worldly hopes (no. 39), it nevertheless felt the need to issue the caution that the proper mission which Christ gave the Church is not 'political, economic or social', but 'religious' (no. 42), quoting Pius XII on the 'strictly religious' goal of the church (note 132). Insofar as 'religious' is understood in an exclusive sense as concerned only with God, and is not seen as penetrating into the depths of the world where the Spirit is at work, and as encompassing the whole of human history in which the Son became flesh, God would become separated from his own incarnate reality.

For God is not merely the creator of the world as something dif-ferent from himself, but rather he 'gives himself away to this world' and 'has his own fate in and with this world':

Only when this statement is made, when, within a concept of God that makes a radical distinction between God and the world, God himself is still the very core of the world's reality and the world is truly the fate of God himself, only then is the concept of God attained that is really Christian.[32]

In the unity of the trinitarian God is encompassed the mystery of God and the mystery of the world together.

Perhaps it was the special genius of Karl Rahner always to have been aware in his theology of the larger picture within which each individual element has its reality and meaning, and to see all things in relationship. We have seen him use the phrase 'differentiated unity' or 'dialectical unity' frequently and in many contexts: between God and the world, between the divine and the human, between transcendence and history, between grace and nature , between salvation history and secular history, between the Church and the world, between knowledge and love, between matter and spirit, between love of God and neighbour, between eschatological hope and worldly hopes, between time and eternity, to name some of them. In each instance the phrases point to the need to relate and understand together elements that we tend to divide and separate. Hence he always looked for the 'prior unity' from out of which distinctions emerge, so that he could understand distinct elements such as divine and human or grace and freedom as 'varying in direct and not indirect proportion'. From this point of view his genius was the ability to synthesize and integrate.

At the same time no detail was too small to fit into the picture, even the 'everyday things' that make up the routine of daily life. We have seen him speak often of the variety and pluralism that form the texture of the larger picture. He did not rush too quickly 'from the many to the one', nor reduce a manifold variety to a single, univocal concept. Instead, a thoroughgoing analogy of being created space for all the contours and textures of the reality he encountered. All of it was important because all of it was God's creation and destined to be part of God's future. Hence each finite reality in its own uniqueness could reveal another facet of the whole, and God could be 'found in all things'. Being able to integrate each part into the whole meant also being able to see the whole in each part.

Because of Rahner's trinitarian vision, that is, because he saw God not just as standing over against the world as the creative origin of all things, but also as dwelling within in his Spirit and as becoming incarnate in history in his Son, and because, therefore, he saw God not just as different from the world but also one with it, he was able to point to all human experience as offering a possible encounter with God. He spoke often of God as incomprehensible mystery, and yet, because it is the mystery of trinitarian love, he was also able to speak of the 'mysticism of everyday things' where God is always close and near at hand in his Word and Spirit. Only such a trinitarian vision of God is one that is really Christian and does justice to the God who was revealed in Jesus Christ.

The mystery of the Trinity is not only the central focus which unifies all the various threads of Rahner's theology, but it also throws light on the spirit which animated his theology. His concern that the Trinity was a 'forgotten truth' on the practical level was basically a pastoral concern. He was convinced that a renewed understanding of the Trinity would serve the practice of faith in the world today. When Karl Rahner first entered the Jesuits he saw himself doing pastoral work as a university chaplain. Though this was never to be and he spent his life as a university professor instead, he never lost his basically pastoral concern. For him the task of theology was ultimately pastoral: to help the people of the Church understand their faith better so that they could live it better, and thus be a sign of the kingdom in the contemporary world.

By identifying the immanent Trinity with the Trinity who are present and active in the world and in history, the most esoteric of doctrines became at once the most pastoral, and the most theoretical of doctrines became at once the most practical. For the Trinity is the deepest revelation of God's sovereign freedom in choosing to love and to be involved in and with the world and humankind as his own. To love God in return, then, is to become associated with him in his freedom and action, to become united with him in his love for the world. Serving God *is* serving the least of his brothers and sisters, and what is done for them *is* done for him (Matt 25:40). This service is not merely the application or the test of one's love for God, but the enactment and realization of this love.

Rahner never tired of saying that God is not known and loved as one object among other objects, indeed not as an object at all, and that God is experienced not just in a separate category of 'religious' experience. God is to be found not only in such 'religious' moments, but in all moments and 'in all things'. 'Things' here refers not primarily to inert objects, but to one's action and interaction and relationship with the world. Karl Rahner learned early on the Ignatian ideal of being a 'contemplative in action', and showed in his theology that action can be contemplation and union with God because it is with God that one is acting. The theoretical task of theology in its search for understanding bears fruit in such action which brings the knowledge of God that comes from doing the truth.

Notes

1 'Observations on the doctrine of God in Catholic dogmatics', TI 9, p. 137.

2 Ibid.

3 'Remarks on the dogmatic treatise "De Trinitate" ', TI 4, p. 85, note 12.

4 'The concept of mystery in Catholic theology', TI 4, p. 36.

5 Ibid., p. 38.

6 Ibid., p. 72.

7 Ibid., p. 69.

8 'Observations on the doctrine of God', p. 143.

9 'Remarks on the dogmatic treatise "De Trinitate" ', pp. 91-2.

10 Ibid., pp. 92-3.

11 Ibid., p. 93.

12 Ibid., p. 94.

13 *The Trinity* (London: Burns & Oates/New York: Herder & Herder, 1970), pp. 34-5.

14 Ibid., p. 36.

15 Ibid., pp. 37-8.

16 Ibid., p. 39.

17 'Observations on the doctrine of God', pp. 133-4.

18 Ibid., p. 134, note 9.

19 Ibid., p. 136.

20 *The Trinity*, pp. 84-5.

21 Ibid., p. 88.

22 Ibid., pp. 91-4.

23 Ibid., pp. 98-9.

24 Ibid., pp. 101-2.

25 'Oneness and three-foldness of God in discussion with Islam', TI 18, p. 109.

26 *The Trinity*, pp. 103-9.

27 Ibid., p. 109.

28 Ibid., pp. 115-20.

29 'The mystery of the Trinity', TI 16, p. 259.

30 'Observations on the doctrine of God', p. 142.

31 *The Trinity*, pp. 10-11.

32 'The specific character of the Christian concept of God', TI 21, p. 191.

Index

Adam 142
Adam, Karl 5
agnosticism 20–1,24
anointing of sick, sacrament
   of 8,123
Anselm 22,39,44
anthropology 65,70,79
apocalyptic 138
apriority, subjective 56
Aquinas, Thomas 1–2,5–7,19,30,
   42–3,47,123
Aristotle 6
atheism 86
Augustine 37,134,156
authority 88,95

baptism 84,86,88,116–17,119,
   121–2,125
base communities 93
becoming 71–2
being 46,65
bishops' conferences 92–3
Bonaventure 5

censorship 12
Chalcedon, Council of 2,66,80
charisms 88,95
charity see love
Christians, annonymous 62,64,86
Christology 61,70,76,153
   ascending 49,59,69,75,79,125
   descending 59,67,69,75,79
   evolutionary 79

existentiell 23,30,61
limits of statements about 67
and resurrection 59; see also
   Jesus Christ, resurrection
transcendental 65–81
see also Jesus Christ
Church 13,79,82–101,116
   catholicity 97
   change in 93–4
   charismatic element 94–5
   collegiality 90
   communication in 96
   dual structure 88,94
   faith 22
   holiness 88,124–5
   institutional or hierarchical
      aspects 90,94
   and Jesus Christ 83–4,88–9
   new forms 93
   obedience in 95
   open 93,95
   prophetic element and
      task 94,105,108–9
   as sacrament 83–6,105,118,160
   and sacraments 121–2
   salvation outside 13,86
   salvation through 85–6
   senses of 83,105
   sinfulness 87–8
   teaching authority 88,91,95
   tensions in 95
   unity 11,96–7
   and world 13,34,85–6,102–15,
      160